D1061692

THE UK HOUSING MARKET

To my parents, with love.

The UK Housing Market

An econometric model

DR CHRISTINE M.E. WHITEHEAD
University of London

SAXON HOUSE | LEXINGTON BOOKS

001766

Published by

SAXON HOUSE, D. C. Heath Ltd.
Westmead, Farnborough, Hants., England.

Jointly with

LEXINGTON BOOKS, D. C. Heath & Co.
Lexington, Mass. U.S.A.

ISBN 347 01005 9
Library of Congress Catalog Card Number 74-15926
Printed in Great Britain
by Unwin Brothers Limited
The Gresham Press, Old Woking, Surrey
A member of the Staples Printing Group

Contents

List of tables

List of figures

Preface

This monograph started life in 1966 as a PhD thesis for the University of London which was completed in 1970. Afterwards I was encouraged by my supervisor Dr Meghnad Desai and by Dr Ian Byatt to continue with the project. This is the result.

The work describes an econometric model of the British private housing market during the post-war period. It is still very much a pilot study but, in time, it is hoped that an extension of this type of analysis could be used for forecasting purposes and to examine in quantitative terms the effects of particular housing policies.

I am exceedingly grateful to Dr Desai and Dr Byatt not only for their initial encouragement but also for their continuing interest, advice and comment. Many others have helped me in the preparation of the study. In particular I would like to thank Professor Michael Bromwich, Mr Robert Gould and Mr David Stanton. I am extremely grateful to the computer unit at LSE, especially Miss Margaret Elliot, for their assistance and patience. I am also indebted to the Department of the Environment for financial and other assistance in the preparation of this study and to the Nationwide Building Society for use of their house price data. Finally and most particularly I would like to thank Mrs Barbara Silver who typed both the thesis and this monograph and has helped enormously throughout the eight years since I first became interested in housing. Of course all the errors and faults remaining are my own.

Goldsmiths College
London School of Economics
May 1974

PART I

The Housing Situation in Great Britain

1 The Housing Stock

1.1 Introduction

In this monograph we examine the workings of the housing market in Great Britain. The main analysis is in the form of a quantitative model in which we look at the determinants of demand, supply and price of new, privately owned, dwellings. In order to set this in its context we first describe in detail the current housing situation and its evolution during the twentieth century. Then we examine the effects of possible changes in govenment policy on the structure of the private housing market with the aid of the quantitative model. In so doing actual government policies and the effects they have had on housing, particularly since 1945, are discussed. Finally we analyse possible changes in policy in the light of the model's forecasts and current government behaviour.

The monograph consists of three sections. The first describes the current housing structure in Great Britain, and its history since the beginning of the twentieth century. In particular it examines the importance of government policy in determining the housing situation. The second section sets out an econometric model of the new, private housing market in Great Britain covering the years 1955–70.[1] It looks at the empirical data available in this country and analyses the structure of demand and supply over the period. In the third section forecasts of future trends in the housing market are analysed and the effects of government behaviour both in relation to the current housing structure and the behaviour of the model are assessed. We conclude by examining some possible changes in policy.

1.2 The housing stock

In section one a general survey of housing in Great Britain is presented. The total stock of houses and additions to the stock since the war are discussed in terms both of quantity and quality. The available stock is compared with housing 'need' where need is defined in terms of a generally recognised judgement of socially acceptable standards of housing. The comparison of 'need' to availability gives an idea of the changing housing

3

situation and the extent to which government objectives are being met. This is in contrast to the discussion in the second section which examines the effects of economic variables on demand and supply for housing in a positive rather than normative manner.

The housing stock in Great Britain has more than doubled since the beginning of the century although the population has only increased by about 20 per cent. Table 1.1 shows the total stock and the stock of houses per 1,000 persons at decade intervals through the century. The figures suggest that the number of persons per dwelling has declined greatly during this period partly as a result of the reduction in multi-occupation and partly because of the decrease in average family size. The rate of increase in stock has varied considerably from decade to decade. Completions fell to near zero during the two world wars, and indeed between 1939 and 1945 the housing stock actually decreased by over 100,000 units. The two major periods of expansion were the early 1930s, when a maximum of 371,000 completed dwellings was reached in 1936 and the mid 1960s, when 426,000 dwellings were completed in 1968. Since then there has been a declining trend in yearly completions with year to year variations. In 1972 only 319,000 new units were added to the stock.

Table 1.1

Changes in the Stock of dwellings in Great Britain

	Stock '000s	Growth rate in previous decade (per cent per annum)	Houses per 1,000 persons	
			Total population	Population over 20
1911	8,814	1·2	214	360
1921	9,400	0·3	212	338
1931	10,597	1·2	237	352
1941		No estimate as no complete census		
1951	13,331	1·3	283	397
1961	16,270	1·7	316	453
1971	18,967	1·5	351	509

Sources: Censuses 1951 and 1961. B.R. Mitchell and P. Deane, *Abstract of British Historical Statistics. Housing and Construction Statistics,* vol. 1, 1973. *Monthly Digest of Statistics,* February 1973.

A major factor affecting the housing situation is the demographic structure of the country. Over the century as a result of wars, changes in the
average ages of marriage and death, family size and other factors, there
have been considerable variations in the rate of household formation. In
particular the low birth rate during the depression and the Second World
War which was immediately followed by a baby boom caused large changes
in demand for housing. In the late 1950s and early 1960s this demand was
increased by net immigration mainly from the new commonwealth.
Changes in social behaviour are also influential: for instance the trend
toward one person households during the post-war period has increased
the demand for separate dwellings significantly. Until recently figures for
household formation, rather than simply crude data on births, marriages
and deaths have not been available, but the Department of the Environment has now produced estimates for the late 1960s and projected them
into the 1970s. They are shown in Table1.2. They suggest that household
formation is beginning to decline now that the children of the post-war
baby boom are generally married. At the same time deaths are increasing
as an echo of the increased survival rate of babies at the beginning of the
century. Both these trends are expected to be reversed by the 1980s. An
increase in the rate of household formation will normally increase the
demand for housing although it is not a one-to-one relationship because

Table 1.2

Household formation in Great Britain ('000s)

	1967	1971	1976
Married new households	373	380	370
Plus immigrant households	56	52	48
Minus emigrant households	80	65	60
Minus deaths causing dissolution	150	168	177
Minus elderly households dissolved for other reasons	37	40	43
Net increase	162	159	138
Other	−2	−9	−13
	160	150	125

Source: *Social Trends,* no. 1, 1970.

not all households are able, or wish, to find separate accomodation immediately. Initial rises in demand for this reason will normally be felt in the
rental market. Any resultant rise in the demand for owner-occupied
housing may well come later in the life-cycle because it takes time for
families to settle down and save enough for the deposit.[2]

Even on crude figures there have not, until possibly very recently, been
enough dwellings for all households. In 1951 there were 14·6 million households in Great Britain and only 14·0 million dwellings, in 1961 16·5
million compared to 16·3 million, and in 1966, 17·8 million compared to
17·5 million. It now appears that the crude deficiency has been overcome
although strictly comparable census statistics for 1971 are not yet available. It is certainly still true that there are fewer dwellings than are needed
when housing need is defined as households plus 4 per cent vacancies to

Table 1.3

Dwellings and housing need — by Region (mid—1971)

	Housing need* (million)	Dwellings (million)	Excess or deficiency (per cent)
England			
Northern	1·16	1·16	—
Yorks and Humber	1·74	1·74	—
North West	2·40	2·36	−2
East Midlands	1·20	1·20	—
West Midlands	1·78	1·73	−3
East Anglia	0·59	0·61	+3
South East	6·07	5·93	−2
Greater London	2·64	2·54	−4
South West	1·35	1·35	—
Total	16·31	16·07	−1
Wales	0·97	0·96	—
Scotland	1·79	1·80	+1
Great Britain	19·06	18·84	−1

* Estimated potential households plus 4 per cent for vacancies and second
houses.

Source: *Social Trends*, no. 3, 1972.

allow for mobility and second homes. No offsetting allowance is made for the possibility of voluntary sharing. The picture varies considerably between different areas of the country, being worst in the major conurbations: London, Birmingham, Manchester and Liverpool. The regional figures are given in Table 1.3 and suggest that even in simple numerical terms the level of housing stock available is inadequate to meet housing 'needs' in the country as a whole let alone area by area.

When we look at the quality of the available accomodation rather than just at numbers the situation is even less impressive. Estimates of the age of the housing stock (Table 1.4) show that over one third of the available dwellings were built before 1918 and nearly 60 per cent before the Second World War. The proportions of each age group vary considerably between regions, being oldest in Wales. These variations reflect the movement of population and the varying rates of slum clearance in different regions. The age distribution of the housing stock suggests that many dwellings must be unsuitable for modern requirements because of the immobile and unchanging nature of the goods, for the size and age distribution of households have changed very greatly leading to changes in the type of housing service required. In particular the number of single person households both young and old has increased very greatly. Also the centres of population have moved in some areas and there has been general migration from the countryside to the major conurbations and from the north to the south. These factors lead to excess supply of some types of housing in particular locations and excess demand for others. Further, as incomes rise the nature of the service required changes. As late as the 1930s houses

Table 1.4

Stock of dwellings by age (December 1971)

Date of construction	Pre 1870 (per cent)	1871–1918 (per cent)	1919–44 (per cent)	Post 1944 (per cent)	Total number '000s (100 per cent)
England	9·3	25·8	24·6	40·3	16,185
Wales	15·7	31·8	15·7	36·8	967
Scotland	5·5	29·9	19·7	44·9	1,815
Great Britain	9·3	26·4	23·7	40·6	18,967

Source: *Housing and Construction Statistics,* vol. I, 1st Quarter, 1972.

were being built with no inside WC and it was not until the 1960s that central heating became an amenity normally provided in new housing. As dwellings are often difficult to modify effectively the age distribution of the existing stock implies that there is likely to be considerable discrepancy between the stock of housing services available and that which is required to meet currently accepted standards of 'need'.

We can examine this further by looking at the data on amenities available in the existing stock. Table 1.5 shows the incidence of lack of the five basic amenities by tenure. Privately rented accommodation, the major component of the category of other tenures, suffers by far the worst provision of basic amenities. This mainly reflects the age structure of this section of the market as well as the general decline of the sector which has resulted from government policy (described in Chapter 4). The great majority of owner-occupied and local council housing have the basic amenities either because they were included when the houses were built or because modernisation and improvement have taken place later, often with the assistance of a government grant. However in 1971 there were still 3·1 million dwellings in England and Wales defined as substandard (unfit or without one of the basic amenities) and it was not expected that even the existing slums would be cleared before 1981. Thus it is unlikely that 'need', when it is defined in both quantity and quality terms, will be met until even later in the century.

Of course none of these comparisons take account of the differences which are likely to occur between demand and 'need'. 'Need' relates to some socially accepted level of housing provision based on the quantity and quality of the available services. It is not necessarily an operational concept because government and individuals may not be prepared to actually spend the money required. The operational variable is not 'need' but demand which takes account of willingness and ability to pay.[3] These will be affected particularly by the relationship between income and house prices and by the nature of government policy towards housing including controls, standards, taxes and subsidies, discussed later.

One of the major differences relating to the housing stock at the present time in comparison to the beginning of this century is the tenure structure. In 1914 the great majority of dwellings, about 90 per cent, were privately let. It was only after the First World War that local authorities started to build many houses to let, and between the wars they built over a quarter of the permanent houses erected in Great Britain, a total of 1,333,000 in comparison to the 3,002,000 built for private owners. Immediately after the Second World War the proportion of dwellings built by local authorities was very high but that proportion fell rapidly in the

Table 1.5

Housing conditions in England and Wales 1971 (per cent)

	Owner-occupied	Rented from LAs and New Towns	Other tenures	All tenures (including closed and vacant)
Dwellings lacking:				
WC inside dwelling	7·8	5·6	31·4	11·9
Fixed bath in a bathroom	5·7	2·2	29·8	9·5
Wash basin	6·9	6·6	32·9	11·9
Sink	0·3	0·2	1·1	0·5
Hot and cold at three points	8·4	7·6	36·9	13·9
One or more of the above	10·9	10·7	40·2	16·8
Total stock '000 dwellings	9,062	4,783	2,821	17,100

Source: Cmnd. 5339, *Better Homes The Next Priorities*, HMSO, June 1973, Table 4.

second half of the 1950s. In 1951 public completions were 89 per cent of new completions but by 1960 this proportion had dropped to 35 per cent. Since then although the numbers of local authority dwellings built have varied very greatly from year to year the proportion has rarely been greater than 50 per cent. In 1972 the proportion was 38 per cent. By 1972 more than 30 per cent of the housing stock was owned by local authorities, a total of over six million homes (see Table 1.6). Most of these have been specifically built by or on contract to local authorities although a few have been bought from private owners, generally to facilitate the rehabilitation or redevelopment of low standard property. The movement has not been entirely one way. Local authorities have sold some council houses to private owner-occupiers but the totals involved have been quite small (see Chapter 4).

Since 1945 local authorities have taken over from the private sector as the main landlords. To a great extent this change was caused by the relative taxation and subsidy structure which penalises privately owned rental property while aiding local authorities and owner-occupation. The continuation of rent control where the legislation has hardly been modified since the First World War has also been an important factor. Indeed, since 1945 very few dwellings have been added to the private rental sector while an enormous number of rented units have been transferred to the owner-occupied sector or have been demolished as part of the slum clear-

Table 1.6

Stock of dwellings: by Tenure, Great Britain

	Owner-occupied (per cent)	Rented from Local Authorities and New Town Corporations (per cent)	Other rented (per cent)		Total (000's)
1947	26	13	61		13,000*
			Private	Other	
1966	46·6	28·4	19·6	5·4	17,468
1972	51·0	30·6	13·4	5·0	19,180

* Estimated.

Sources: P.G. Gray, 'The British Household — The Social Survey 1949'. *Housing and Construction Statistics,* no. 5, 1st Quarter, 1973, Table XI.

10

ance programme. Some new construction has entered the sector via luxury flats for rental, which are not affected by rent controls. But most of the dwellings that have come into the private rental sector since the 1930s are conversions to increase the number of dwelling units in a given structure (a large proportion which occurred during wartime to offset the housing shortage). As a result the proportion of total stock which is privately rented has declined until in 1971 it was only 13·4 per cent, a fall of about six million units since 1914.

The growth of owner-occupation began between the wars although the major expansion in numbers has taken place since 1946. The proportion of the total stock which is owner-occupied has almost doubled since 1945 to just over 50 per cent in 1971, a total of almost 9·5 million homes. This growth has been aided enormously by specialist financial intermediaries providing capital for house purchase, and by large implicit subsidies to owner-occupiers from central government. At the current time the predictions are that the proportion of stock in owner-occupation is likely to increase further while the proportion of private rental property will continue to decline.[4]

The size of the housing stock is modified in three ways — by new building, by demolitions and by conversions. Completions, by far the most important of these, as we have already discussed, increase the stock by varying amounts up to 2 per cent per annum. On the other hand demolitions for slum clearance and for other reasons such as road building can be as much as 0·5 per cent per annum, while an unknown number of houses are converted and in the process extra dwelling units may be added. A fairly conservative estimate would be that there was a net increase in stock of about 1·5 per cent per annum during the 1950s and early 1960s but this has fallen in the latter half of the 1960s to about 1·1 per cent in 1972. There is surprisingly little information about pre-war demolitions and almost nothing about conversions. Paige estimated that there were between 2 and 2·2 million demolitions in the century 1861 to 1961 of which nearly one million took place before 1931.[5] She also estimated that just under one million dwelling units were converted between 1861 and 1961, between 550,000 and 650,000 of which took place after 1931.

The nature of the overall changes in stock since the war are shown in Table 1.7. These figures include the Department of the Environment's own estimates of 'other' gains and losses. The 'other' gains are never more than 4 per cent of total gains even at the height of the post-war conversion boom. 'Other' losses on the other hand are far more significant being as high as one third of all losses in the early 1950s and even in 1971 the proportion was well over 20 per cent. This is accounted for mainly by

11

Table 1.7

Stock of dwellings: estimated gains and losses, Great Britain ('000s)

	Gains		Losses		Net gain	Stock at end of period
	New construction	Other	Slum clearance	Other		
1951–55 (annual average)	283·8	10·1	31·4	15·7	246·8	15,146
1956–60 (annual average)	290·0	10·8	66·9	20·3	273·6	16,215
1966	385·5	6·6	87·1	32·8	272·2	17,660
1972	319·1	10·3	88·8	27·1	213·6	19,180

Source: *Housing & Construction Statistics*, no. 5, 1st Quarter 1973, Table X.

large scale urban renewal which usually includes many non slum dwellings, and by transportation schemes. This type of demolition is expected to increase in the future.

Slum clearance is the main element included in losses. These are the result of local government action taken with the help of central government subsidies. The real value of these subsidies varies considerably be-

Table 1.8

Total dwellings demolished or closed, Great Britain

	England and Wales	Scotland
1951	11450	
1952	11090	
1953	14487	
1954	18635	
1955	24373	10546[e]
1956	34336	12095[e]
1957	44515	12167[e]
1958	52623	13379[e]
1959	57553	13358[e]
1960	56561	12285[e]
1961	61969	11749[e]
1962	62431	12085
1963	61445	12058
1964	68215	14392
1965	60666	15534
1966	66782	16650
1967	71152	19087
1968	71586	18768
1969	69233	17847
1970	67804	17345
1971	70057	20554
1972	66098	18518

[e] estimated.

Sources: England and Wales: *Housing Statistics,* no. 9, Table 33. Scotland: *Housing Statistics,* no. 9, Table 36. *Housing and Construction Statistics,* no. 5, Tables 32, 33.

tween local authorities (depending mainly upon their past building behaviour) and over time. Local authorities have very different incentives towards slum clearance depending upon the general housing situation, the quality of the stock in their neighbourhood and the political complexion of the local authority. As a result, the level of slum clearance varies very greatly over the country, being proportionately very much higher in Scotland than in England and Wales. The rate of slum clearance also fluctuates from year to year reflecting the general level of activity in the economy as well as the size of central government subsidy. Table 1.8 sets out the number of dwelling units lost through slum clearance since 1951. The current estimates show that in terms of currently accepted standards there are still nearly one million designated slums in Great Britain and another two and a half million lacking at least one basic amenity.[6] Because of this substandard nature of the stock demolitions are likely to continue, probably at much the same rate as currently, until at least the turn of the century.[7]

The most important component of changes in stock is the number of new completions. Chart 1.1 shows housing starts and completions since 1954. There is a very strong seasonal variation both in starts and completions with starts highest in the second quarter and completions highest in the fourth quarter in the private sector. In the public sector both are high in the second and third quarters. Starting around 320,000 per annum in

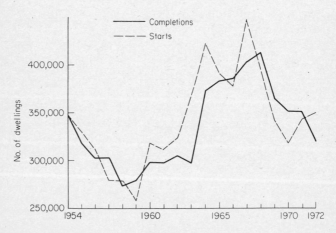

Fig. 1.1   Total housing starts and completions (1954–72)

Sources: *Housing Statistics*
Housing and Construction Statistics
each issue: 'House building Performance'

14

1954 the rate of completions fell considerably in the late 1950s to little over 260,000 in 1958. Local authority housing was cut back and the private sector, although increasing steadily and rapidly was not able to offset this and keep up the total rate of increase in the housing stock. In the early 1960s, however, building for local authorities increased again for a while but since the middle of the decade it has fallen steadily. Private sector building also fell in the later 1960s from a maximum of 222,000 in 1968 to 196,000 in 1972 so that overall total completions fell back from a high of 414,000 in 1968 to 319,000 in 1972. In 1974 housing activity is expected to be no higher and over the whole period it has been rare for government targets of new building to be met. The large year to year fluctuations suggest that the building industry is very sensitive to changes in the national activity level as are the local authorities; the reasons for this will be discussed in detail in relation to the econometric model set out in section two of this monograph.

We have already discussed the quantity of the existing stock. We look next at the quality of new housing where the evidence suggests that it has been improving consistently and that minimum standards have been increasing throughout the century. Paige[8] estimated the cost of building a typical house at intervals throughout the previous century at 1962 prices

Table 1.9

Replacement cost of typical houses at 1962 prices

Year of construction	Floor area sq. ft	Total replacement cost	£ 1962 per sq. ft
1840	435	700	1·61
1880	625	1200	1·92
1890	625	1225	1·96
1905	672	1250	1·86
1920	705	1375	1·95
1925	755	1500	1·99
1937	760	1700	2·11
1947	800	1875	2·34
1952	825	2025	2·45

Source: Paige in W. Beckerman and others, *The British Economy in 1975*, Cambridge University Press, 1965, Chapter 12.

in an attempt to produce an index of quality. Her results, set out in Table 1.9, suggest that the average size of house has almost doubled in a hundred years as has the quality of materials used and amenities provided.[9] There have been no official published estimates of changes in quality since the war to extend this attempt but some sources suggest that the quality of new housing has been increasing at about 4 per cent per annum.[10] Certainly garages and central heating have become normal amenities during the post-war period.

Apart from the available quantity and quality another important aspect of the housing situation is the amount people have to pay for their accomodation both in absolute terms and in relation to their income. So we turn next to an examination of the prices at which new and existing supply is available. The general belief is that prices of houses in the owner-occupied sector are always rising. This view is not backed up by the data. During the last hundred years house prices have certainly not always increased more rapidly than the general price level and between the wars particularly house prices fell quite considerably. However, since 1945, the belief is generally upheld by the data, for prices have increased rapidly and faster than general prices, especially in the last few years. The movement of house prices over the century compared with prices in general is given in Table 1.10. The figures suggest that house prices have varied more than general prices and appear to have taken off since 1955. The relative situation has got worse since 1968, even in comparison to the generally increased rate of inflation. The greatest increase came between 1970 and 1973 when new house prices rose about 85 per cent but there are now signs of quite a large decline in house prices at least in some areas.

The available figures are not, however, normalised for quality, an important factor in relation to such a heterogeneous product as housing. We have already suggested that quality has been generally increasing. If this is true the increases in the relative price of housing will be overstated to the extent that quality has increased more in housing than in the whole range of goods covered by general prices indices.

The alternative to owner-occupation is to rent either from local authorities or furnished or unfurnished from private owners. It is extremely difficult to obtain comprehensive information on the trends in private rents.[11] Until 1973 many rents had been controlled at 1939 levels with some increase for repair costs allowed since the war. In the inter-war period large numbers of dwellings were controlled at the 1914 level but as general prices were constant or falling controlled rents did not differ very greatly from uncontrolled rents by the mid 1930s. 'Fair rents' which do not take account of shortage but are generally higher than controlled rents began to be introduced in 1965 but the process will not be complete until 1975. [12] The price of uncontrolled private rented dwellings, which include all furnished accomodation and some high-quality unfurnished accomodation, has risen since the Second World War reflecting not only general cost and price rises but also acute shortages in some areas particularly London and the other large conurbations. The Francis Committee for instance found that 'the furnished sector pays higher rents for inferior accomodation (as measured by gross annual value) particularly in the stress areas.' This 'is not due to the occupation of more rooms but can only relate to the fact of the tenancy being furnished.' [13]

Our main source of comparative information between tenures comes from the Family Expenditure Survey which has been published annually since the mid-1960s. Members of the sample keep detailed records of their expenditure over a two-week period. Although the results are biased for certain types of spending particularly expenditure on liquor and tobacco,

Table 1.10

The price of owner-occupied housing compared to general prices 1900−70

	Consumer expenditure average value index (1963 = 100)	Prices of existing housing (1963 = 100)
1900	17·1	11
1914	19·8	11
1920	50·8	33
1930	34·8	20
1939	34·8	21
1946	54·0	45
1950	65·4	61
1955	81·5	61
1960	91·8	77
1965	108·0	124
1968	120·1	136
1970	131·3	171

Source: *The British Economy Key Statistics, 1900−70*, London and Cambridge, 1972.

there is no reason to expect any major inexactitude in the housing expenditure figures. However, because of the small proportion of the sample that occupy privately rented furnished accommodation, no figures are published for that sector.

Table 1.11 shows annual rents and mortgage payments and the proportion of income spent on housing in 1970. House purchases are made by the richer section of the population. This is reflected in the evidence that they pay roughly twice as much as local authority tenants for housing but the proportion of income entailed is only about 10 per cent greater. The figures do not really reflect true costs to the average home-owner because about half of the 9·5 million owner-occupied dwellings are owned in full, while some higher priced dwellings are paid for by insurance methods. No attempt is made to estimate their costs. Also figures of this kind cannot reflect the real difference between paying throughout one's life without obtaining a property right, as in the rental sector, against finally owning

Table 1.11

Rebated rents and mortgage payments, Great Britain 1970

Annual payment £ p.a.	Local authority (per cent)	Private unfurnished (per cent)	Owner-occupiers with reducing mortgages (per cent)
Under £ 20 ⎱	2	⎰ 4 ⎱	
20 – ⎰		⎱ 22 ⎰	4
40 –	7	21 ⎰	
60 –	13	13	4
80 –	18	9	11
100 –	34	10	12
140 –	22	10	23
200 – ⎱	4	10	⎰ 22
300 and over ⎰			⎱ 24
Mean	115	98	232
Median	111	64	210
Percentage of household income			
Mean	9·5	10·0	10·9
Median	7·7	6·9	9·9
Percentage of head of household income			
Mean	13·6	11·8	14·0
Median	11·0	9·1	12·3
SAMPLE BASE	1,936	897	1,416

Source: Family Expenditure Survey 1970.

one's own capital asset as in the owner-occupied sector.

The private unfurnished rental sector shows a different distribution of rents in comparison to the other tenures. There are still a large number of very low rents which have not yet come under the 'fair rent' legislation and so reflect modified 1939 values. However, as 'fair rents' become the norm we would expect private sector rents to become more comparable to local authority rents taking into account that quality is generally lower.

Rents and house prices as a proportion of income differ not only between tenures but also between areas. On average in 1972 households in the UK spent £4·42 per week on housing which is about 12·6 per cent of household expenditure. In Greater London the proportion was higher at 14·8 per cent (£6·25 as against £42·18 expenditure). In the rest of England the proportion ranges from about 12 per cent to 13·5 per cent but in Scotland it is only 10·5 per cent, while in Northern Ireland it is relatively very low at 7·7 per cent.[14] These figures to some extent reflect different proportions of households buying their own homes and also different housing qualities, but they also show up real variations in the burden of expenditure on accomodation on household standards of living. Over the last couple of years as inflation and house prices have increased more rapidly it is probable that the variation around these means has also increased because the difference between the price of new contracts and ones negotiated in the past have become greater. In particular the real costs of financing first-purchase have markedly increased in comparison to buying a house when one is already an owner-occupier and has the capital gain on the earlier dwelling to use as a down payment on the new house.

So far we have discussed a number of factors relating to the housing stock in some detail. We turn next to an analysis of the house building industry and its effectiveness in adding new dwellings to the available stock.

Notes

[1] As 1954 was the last year in which many of the wartime controls were in operation, that initial date marks the earliest time that there was a free building industry. The model covers Great Britain, and so excludes Northern Ireland where the housing market is rather different.

[2] The average age of first-purchase is said by the Building Societies' Association to be about thirty, while the average age of marriage is about twenty-four for men.

[3] This point is discussed in relation to London's housing problems in

C. D. Foster and C. M. E. Whitehead, 'The Layfield Report on the Greater London Development Plan', *Economica*, November 1973, vol. XL, no. 160, pp. 442–54.

[4] This is still true in the longer term. In the short term, however, it is expected that the rate of growth of owner-occupation will be slowed by high interest rates and credit controls.

[5] See Chapter 12 of W. Beckerman and others, *The British Economy in 1975*, Cambridge University Press, 1965.

[6] See *Better Homes: The Next Priorities*, Cmnd 5339, published by HMSO for the Department of the Environment and the Welsh Office, 1973.

[7] Current movement towards rehabilitation rather than clearance may cut these losses but is unlikely to affect the demolition of designated slums.

[8] In W. Beckerman and others, op. cit.

[9] Vera Hole in 'Housing Standards and Social Trends', *Urban Studies*, November 1965, vol. 2, no. 2, discusses minimum standards prescribed in official handbooks since 1918. She suggests there has been an upward, though uneven, trend in quality throughout the period. The Parker Morris Report, *Homes for To-day and To-morrow* a report of a subcommittee of the Central Housing Advisory Committee (1961) set standards for new local authority housing which required increased space, better quality and equipment. The report has been implemented to some extent and the upward trend in quality is expected to continue, although many private dwellings are still built below Parker Morris standards.

[10] Oral communication with the Department of the Environment.

[11] The main sources of information on private rents have been interview surveys by government and others. See for example private surveys by J. B. Cullingworth, *Housing in Transition*, Heineman, 1963; J. Greve, 'Private Landlords in England', Occasional Paper in Social Administration, no. 16, 1965; J. Carmichael, 'Vacant Possession', Institute of Economic Affairs, Hobart Paper no. 28, 1964. The two main government surveys are P. G. Gray, and R. Russell, *The Housing Situation in 1960*, SS 319, and M. Woolf, *The Housing Situation in England and Wales in 1964*, SS 372, and the *Report of the Committee on the Rent Acts* (the Francis Committee) Cmnd, 4609, 1971. *The Milner Holland Report*, Cmnd, 2605, 1965 surveyed rents in Greater London.

[12] The concept of a 'fair rent' and its effect on rental levels is discussed in detail in Chapter 4.

[13] Report of the committee on the Rent Acts, op. cit., p. 131.

[14] Source: Family Expenditure Survey 1972.

2 The Construction Industry

2.1 The structure of the industry

Investment in housing is a large proportion of overall investment taking over 4 per cent of gross domestic product at its post-war maximum in 1968 although since then the proportion has been declining as both private and public housing activity have contracted. Table 2.1 shows the trends since the early 1960s reflecting in particular the varying importance of the public and private sectors. If we look at investment in dwellings in relation to overall capital formation it is of course a much larger proportion. It also varies less suggesting that investment in dwellings moves cyclically with all other investment. In 1968, the peak year for housing completions, investment was 20 per cent of gross domestic capital formation, while in 1971 it had fallen to 17 per cent. In 1972 the proportions were roughly similar. [1] These figures are based on value in current prices so they do not take account of the possible relative increase in price and factor costs of housing, a point which we examine in more detail later in the chapter. Yet however it is measured we must regard housing as an important part of the economic activity of the economy. But although the

Table 2.1

Gross domestic fixed capital formation in housing in the UK (£m)

	1962	1965	1968	1971
At current prices				
Public sector	344	558	816	766
Private sector	512	674	736	845
Total	856	1232	1552	1611
Percentage GDP at factor cost	3·44	4·00	4·22	3·37

Source: *Housing and Construction Statistics,* no. 2, 2nd Quarter, 1972, Table VIII.

industry is so large and influential its structure has changed little over the last decades, its methods of production are still mainly the traditional processes and there seems little sign of technical change.

Even in simple terms it is extremely difficult to give a clear account of the house building industry because most of the available data covers the construction industry as a whole rather than the housing sector alone. Indeed it is only the investment figures which clearly relate specifically to housing. The construction industry as a whole is typified in Britain by a large number of small firms with extremely low capitalisation. Regular figures on the structure of the industry have only been available since the beginning of the 1960s but the general picture is of an industry with a declining number of firms and yet little sign of increasing firm size. Table 2.2 shows the number of firms in the industry in 1965 and 1970. It does not reflect any very clear trends in industrial structure, if anything suggesting a decline in the number of larger firms. Before 1965 the figures are not strictly comparable as they were given in terms of operatives rather than employees — but to the extent that they can be assessed

Table 2.2

Structure of the construction industry

| No. of employees | 1965 | | 1970 | |
	(1) No. of firms	(2) Employment of operatives ('000s)	(3) No. of firms	(4) Employment of operatives ('000s)
0–1	18,488	–	20,355	–
2–7	38,774	85·4	33,118	63·5
8–13	10,581	82·2	7,946	60·1
14–24	7,164	107·1	5,358	77·1
25–34	2,648	64·9	1,982	46·9
35–59	2,798	108·1	2,062	75·9
60–79	894	52·8	720	40·6
80–114	790	64·4	616	47·4
115–299	1,040	158·0	820	115·9
300–599	290	100·4	233	72·5
600–1,199	149	120·9	132	83·7
1,200 and over	80	201·8	78	190·6
Total	83,696	1128·0	73,420	874·3

Source: *Housing and Construction Statistics 2*, 2nd Quarter, 1972, Tables II and IV.

a similar picture emerges. If we look instead at the number of operatives by firm size (columns 2 and 4) there appears to be no strong movement towards the larger firms employing comparatively more labour. These figures do not show up the major structural change that has actually taken place in the industry in the 1960s which has been the growth in single person units. This is because these are not normally included in the industry census. This 'labour-only subcontracting' type of employment in the construction industry has grown mainly as the result of changes in the tax laws and the effects of incomes, policy. The introduction of Selective Employment Tax in 1966 was perhaps the basis of the movement for it increased immensely the incentive to be self-employed. General methods of tax assessment and collection further increase these incentives especially in a period of inflation. As a result there are large discrepancies between figures on employment in the construction industry gathered from different sources and so no certainty about overall employment levels.[2] All that can be said for sure is that, excepting self-employment, there is a secular decline in employment in the industry and no very obvious increases in average size of firms. Many firms in the industry are involved in the whole range of construction and civil engineering activity and it is often not possible to separate out that information which relates particularly to housing. Further we cannot regard housing as a normal subsection of the construction industry because other types of construction such as offices, industrial plant, hospitals, schools, roads, etc., involve very much more plant and machinery, and usually involve more prefabrication and industrialised building than housing. Capitalisation and processes are both very different. We can probably assume that most of the larger firms are involved not mainly in house building but in these more capital intensive forms of construction. House building makes up about one third of the construction industry and is done mainly by craftsmen with traditional materials and few tools. Principal contractors or speculative builders often act simply as entrepreneurs collecting together the right skills at the right time but employing labour-only sub-contractors to do most of the specialist work. Capital expenditure per worker per annum is less than one half of the average for manufacturing industry at £74 per worker in 1966.[3] This figure again relates to the whole of the construction industry so we can presume that it is far lower for house building. Low fixed costs and many available alternative uses for labour in repairs, improvement and other areas of construction mean that house-building firms have little incentive to remain in business if work is hard to come by. There is very rapid entry into and exit from the industry and a very high bankruptcy rate. The small, usually local, firms which make up the industry depend on short-term bank finance during building (using the land and part-complete buildings as collateral) and as a result are strongly affected by general monetary policy. Because of the apparently high risks of failure banks are inclined to cut finance to builders early in a squeeze and not to start financing again until money is relatively easy. The private sector house-building industry thus expands and contracts cyclically with the central government's attempts to control inflation. As a result output is likely to vary greatly from year to year. This problem is discussed in more detail in the next chapter on finance.

In the private sector most building is of traditional types in traditional materials. The proportion of industrialised building has always been very small indeed partly because building societies will not easily mortgage such dwellings. In the public sector on the other hand, industrialised building has made up as much as 40 per cent of the total output, mainly in the form of flats. In the last two years the proportion of industrialised building in the local authority sector has fallen again, because of the fall in the proportion of flats to 26 per cent in 1972. This change occurred part-ly because of the accident at Ronan Point but there has also been a general movement away from high-rise buildings on social grounds. Al-though, especially in the large conurbations, there is thus varying local authority demand for industrialised building and therefore for specialist capital equipment there are still plenty of contracts for traditionally built public sector housing which are normally erected by local firms who may also be involved in private speculative building. To some extent public sector house building is not as cyclical as building in the private sector as it depends more on the political structure of central and local government. Yet the public sector is also very dependent upon the ability of local government to raise finance and this is to a great extent determined by central government monetary policy. Further, local authorities are general-ly poor payers in terms of timing so that builders often have to finance most of their work themselves and so run into their own borrowing diffi-culties.[4] As a result although building decisions are based on very differ-ent factors in the public and private sectors, activity is likely to move together to some degree – except perhaps at the top of the market when shortage of labour and materials is likely to lead contractors to concen-trate on private sector building where greater profits can be made.

Builders also vary their level of production by increasing and decreasing construction times. Although the technology of building means that a house need not take more than six weeks to complete the average time taken from start to completion is nearer a year. In the private sector this time varies as the level of activity in the industry and the ease of sale changes. On the other hand, in the public sector, since the war there has been a secular increase in building time from around eleven months for houses to nearly seventeen months. This can partly be explained by the increasing size of contracts and perhaps by more complex building processes. Flats have always taken longer to build than houses because a large number of units are started and finished together. The length of building time is again a function of the small-scale nature of the industry and the subcontracting methods of production which mean that there is little cost attached to building slowly.

The general picture is one of a large number of small firms with rapidly changing composition grouping together and separating again in response to changes in demand. When demand is slack they move into repairs and maintenance, and there is also the close substitute of other types of construction work. The whole structure of the house-building industry is thus extremely fluid.

The main components of the cost of building a house are materials, wages and land. Until lately it has been difficult to obtain data on land costs. The only published source was the *Estates Gazette* which publishes weekly lists of prices of land sold at auction. P. A. Stone of the Building Research Centre worked on this material over the period 1954 − 64.[5] He found enormous variations in prices and these appeared to depend mainly upon the distance from the centre of the nearest conurbation and the adequacy of transport to this point. Because of the enormous differences in individual plot prices and the relevance of particular types of planning permission in determining these prices the Department of the Environment has been slow to publish figures on land prices. They finally produced a series in 1968 which they have now back-dated to 1962. This is reproduced in Table 2.3. The data suggest that in the last ten years prices per plot have increased by 300 per cent while house prices in the same period have only increased by 150 per cent. The great relative expansion in land prices has come mainly in the last two years especially in 1972 and there now appears to be some sign of prices falling. It is suggested that the enormous rise happened because the general speeding up of inflation makes real assets, particularly land, relatively valuable. Expectations of future land values lead to current price increases.[6] It is probable that one reaction to land price rises has been a decrease in average plot size, but there is no continuing published data available to back up this impression. Builders' ability to react in this way is very restricted by local planning controls. In order to build at all the local authority must give planning permission on the basis of long-term general land-use plans. This determines whether any building can be erected at all, whether it can be residential, the density at which dwellings can be built and type of units to be erected. The process, which includes procedures for objections from the public, appeals to county and central authorities and other formalities, can take a very long time and increase the cost and difficulties for the builder. Central government policies are also important through, for example, the 'Green Belt' policy which disallows development of any kind on a large band of land around many conurbations. As a result land is kept artificially scarce, and prices remain high, in order to provide open space and a better environment for the general public.

There are no published data which allow us to determine for certain what proportion of the total cost of a dwelling is accounted for by land costs. Estimates are available for local authority sector building since 1963. Before that date the last official figures were given by the Institute of Municipal Treasurers and Accountants in 1955.[7] These showed the cost of land as only about 2·5 per cent of the total capital cost of the average dwelling, although it was realised that there were extreme variations, because local authorities were unable to obtain cheap land in large conurbations. Needleman [8] in 1965 suggested that for public authorities land costs were far less important than site clearing costs. At that time these

Table 2.3

Land costs and house prices, private sector (1966 = 100)

	Land price per plot England and Wales	Average price of new dwellings mortgaged with building societies
1963	74	79
1964	84	85
1965	94	93
1966	100	100
1967	102	106
1968	118	112
1969	147	120
1970	150	127
1971	185	143
1972	305	184

Source: *Housing and Construction Statistics 4,* 4th Quarter 1972, Table 3.

could be at least four times the cost of land. However, in central areas he estimated that land costs could be up to one third of the total cost of a house.

Cost estimates since 1964 are given in Table 2.4. They show that costs not directly related to land and direct construction are still relatively important being on average nearly twice the land cost in England and Wales. Even split this way, the figures are sure to mask very great differences within the designated areas but suggest that the disparity in land costs between Greater London and the rest of England and Wales is growing larger and land costs in the scarcity areas are becoming increasingly more important.

Turning next to post-war prices for house-building materials we find that since 1957 when comparable figures become available, house-building materials' prices have been going up on a fairly steady trend in comparison

Table 2.4

Average cost of local authority dwellings

	Dwelling construction £	Land acquisition costs*‡ £	Estimated other costs*† £	Estimated average total cost £
England and Wales				
1964	2,390	240	510	3,149
1968	3,180	420	740	4,340
1971	3,590	590	960	5,140
Greater London				
1964	3,110	630	850	4,590
1968	4,090	1,300	1,190	6,580
1971	4,500	1,800	1,150	7,450
Rest of England and Wales				
1964	2,250	190	444	2,884
1968	2,930	300	610	3,840
1971	3,270	400	880	4,550

* Subject to substantial error.
† Ancillary buildings, fees and site works.
‡ Assuming two year lag between acquisition and tender.

Source: *Housing and Construction Statistics*, no. 2, 2nd Quarter, 1972, Table XXII.

27

with other basic materials where prices actually fell in the late 1950s (see Table 2.5). Since devaluation in 1967 house-building materials have been going up more slowly than manufacturing materials until the great house price increase in the 1970s. The slower rate presumably reflects the smaller proportion of building materials that are imports. As a result housing costs are far more affected by internal inflation than by fluctuations in the exchange rate and our terms of trade. House-building costs also appear to have gone up very considerably slower than overall new construction costs suggesting that their relative importance in total output has fallen as a result of changes in technology and possibly in productivity.

Figures available on the costs of labour all refer to the construction industry as a whole. They suggest that weekly earnings of employees have kept pace with those for all industries (Table 2.6) but have certainly not increased more rapidly. At the same time the hours worked are always higher than in industry as a whole and apparently more variable in response to fluctuations in the level of economic activity. These figures must be assessed with care because of the enormous increase in self-employment in the 1960s as there is likely to be an increasing bias because self-employed earnings are not included in the available data. If we wish to assess the effects of changes in labour costs on housing supply we must

Table 2.5

Costs of house building compared with other prices (1963 = 100)

	House-building materials	Basic materials and timber manufacturing industry	New construction output	All manufactured products
1957	91·9	104·5	90	91·5
1960	93·3	99·0	90	93·7
1964	103·3	104·1	102	102·7
1966	109·7	107·9	111	109·5
1968	110·1	117·3	118	116·7
1970	123·7	128·2	131	129·8
1972	146·5	140·0	161	149·0

Source: *Monthly Digest of Statistics,* April 1973, Table 170.

assume that self-employed earnings are higher than employee earnings. The quoted figures will therefore be biased downwards; for if employees earnings were higher than those obtained from self-employment, labour only-subcontractors would be expected to move back into normal employment. Another possibility is that because self-employment is more risky we would expect the variability in hours worked to be understated.

On the face of it greater increases in building costs than in general costs cannot be explained on the basis of increases in labour costs. However, to examine this fully we should also assess comparative changes in labour productivity.

The *Index of Industrial Production* shows that over the post-war period construction has grown less fast than output in general and suffers from greater variability. This is suggested by the data in Table 2.7. However these figures are not normalised for changes in employment (which has been declining in the construction industry) and cannot on their own be regarded as a measure of productivity. Further they do not reflect any differences between changes in efficiency in house building rather than in

Table 2.6

Hours and earnings

	Construction*		All industries	
	Average weekly earnings (Oct.)	Average weekly hours worked	Average weekly earnings (Oct.)	Average weekly hours worked
1948	£ 6·53	47·1	£ 6·90	46·7
1955	£10·78	49·5	£11·15	48·9
1959	£13·02	49·8	£13·54	48·5
1965	£19·77	49·8	£19·58	47·0
1968	£22·87	47·8	£23·00	46·4
1971	£30·11	47·2	£30·93	44·7

* Over the period there have been a number of changes in the standard industrial classification. These figures are therefore not strictly comparable but the differences appear negligible.

Source: *British Labour Statistics Historical Abstract and Yearbooks*, (Various tables).

the construction industry as a whole. The relatively small changes in methods of production in house building suggest that productivity increases may be less than in the industry as a whole. In 1968 the Phelps-Brown Committee stated 'the ordinary quoted increase in productivity or output per man of 4 − 5 per cent annually overstates the true position in that numbers of men are normally understated.'[9] We have no reason to believe that the basis of this assessment has changed greatly since 1968. Because of lack of data, we are really unable to make any statement about the changes in productivity in house building but cannot assume that it has increased any faster than in the rest of the economy.[10]

Some qualitative evidence exists that whatever the rate of change in productivity the average level is relatively low. Certainly this was the opinion of the National Economic Development Council in 1968. In their report[11] Mr. K. M. Wood, Chairman of Concrete Ltd, is quoted as saying

> The most horrifying thing to me is it tends to be a casual industry. The first thing a contractor has to do with a new job os often to hire a site agent. The whole organisation is built up and is just about running well when the contract is finished and the whole cycle starts again. I think anyone who as I do spends a good deal of time halfway between manufacturing production or working on building sites realises the enormous advantages of keeping teams of people working together.

At the same time evidence was put forward that labour productivity in the public sector is even less than in the private sector at roughly 0·9 dwellings per operative per annum against 1·2 dwellings in the private sector. These figures apply to 1965 but the gap was felt to have remained relatively constant since the war.

Our discussion suggests that neither building materials nor labour costs can be regarded as major factors in the relative price increases of both

Table 2.7

Index of industrial production (1963 = 100)

	1954	1957	1960	1963	1966	1968	1970	1972
Construction	83·1	91·0	92·1	100·0	115·3	121·8	115·7	121·7
All industries	79·1	85·0	88·3	100·0	113·2	119·8	124·1	126·8

Source: *Annual Abstract of Statistics,* Tables 163 (1971), 167 (1973).

speculative and local authority housing in comparison to general prices except to the extent that increases in productivity have been overstated. Such a conclusion might suggest that building profits have been increasing as house prices rise but this hypothesis takes no account of the importance of land and clearing costs. Before we could come to any final conclusion as to who gains, tests to determine the relation between land and house prices should he attempted. Theoretically, to the extent that land supply is inelastic we expect excess profit to go to the land-owner and developer rather than to the builder. We have little detailed empirical evidence on this partly because many builders are also land-owners but also because most house-building firms and land-owners are not public limited companies and so do not have to present accounts.

Yet the variability in housing starts and in, for instance, plot sizes does not suggest that either new housing or land is in completely inelastic supply. Other costs such as labour, materials and the costs of financing building are also important. Perhaps in the short run the most important factor is the cost and availability of credit both to builders and house purchasers. We discuss this in the next chapter.

This discussion of the building industry and costs of construction has suggested a number of important determining variables and possible hypotheses to be tested. We will hope to take this further when we come to setting up the econometric model.

Notes

[1] See Table 322 of the *Annual Abstract of Statistics 1973*, Gross Domestic Fixed Capital Formation at Current Prices.

[2] This problem is discussed in detail in the *Phelps-Brown Committee Report to the National Board for Prices and Incomes,* Cmnd 3714, July 1968.

[3] Capital expenditure per annum per worker in the manufacturing industry was £164 — see p. 10 of *Pay and Conditions in the Building Industry*, Cmnd 3837, November 1968.

[4] See J. Parry-Lewis and D. D. Singh, 'Goverment Policy and the Building Industry', *District Bank Review*, June 1966.

[5] See e.g. P. A. Stone, The Price of Building Sites in Britain in P. Hall, *Land Values*, Sweet and Maxwell, London, 1965, and P.A. Stone, 'Housing, Town Development Land and Costs', London, *Estates Gazette*, 1963.

[6] For a discussion of the reasons for increases in the price of land see R.V. Turvey, *The Economics of Real Property*, Allen and Unwin, London,

1957 and 'The Rationale of Rising Property Values', *Lloyds Bank Review No. 63*, 1962.

[7] *Housing Statistics 1954 — 5*, Institute of Municipal Treasurers and Accountants.

[8] L. Needleman, *The Economics of Housing*, Staples Press, London, 1965, pp. 107 — 8.

[9] 'Pay and Conditions in the Building Industry' , *National Board for Prices and Incomes, Report No. 92*, Cmnd 3837, 1968, para. 61.

[10] An early discussion of productivity in house building and likely changes in that productivity and methods of construction can be found in L. Needleman, 'A Long Term View of Housing', *National Institute Economic Review, No. 18*, 1961, and 'Productivity in House Building', *Lloyds Bank Review, No. 69*, 1963.

[11] 'The Building Industry and the Public Client' , Economic Development Committee for Building, NEDC 1968.

3 Financing the Housing Sector

3.1 Introduction

Because of its nature housing requires a complex financing system to assist both demand and supply. This is because it is a durable good which takes a long time to build and, for the individual, a long time to buy.

On the demand side, the growth of the peculiarly British financial institution, the building society, has been successful in aiding the relatively well-off purchaser to buy good quality housing. The system is now perhaps beginning to break down under the twin strain of the unexpected increases in the rate of inflation and the government sponsored extension of competition between the main financial institutions. In the past, however, except for short periods of general credit restriction, the financing of demand has been regarded as relatively successful.

On the supply side the situation is very different. In the house-building industry the overwhelming predominance of small, low-capitalised firms with few financial resources of their own means that the average firm is a risky enterprise dependent upon outside finance. Because of this the house-building industry is strongly affected by the economy's general monetary climate. This helps to produce both great variations in the construction rate and long lags between the creation of new demand resulting from the expansions in incomes and demand credit and the actual provision of new completed houses. Thus financing problems often exacerbate short-term excesses of demand and this appears to lead to rapid price rises rather than to increased supply.

3.2 The financing of demand

Since the beginning of the century owner-occupation has increased from a tiny proportion to over 50 per cent of the total housing market. This has meant the growth of complex financing processes, for the purchase of a house is probable the largest capital outlay that most families undertake in their lifetime. Very roughly the average price of a house is between two and a half and three times purchasers' average income and so they are likely to have to borrow a large amount of outside finance.[1] The main

33

source of such finance in Britain is the building societies. These are non-profit making friendly societies who act as intermediaries between small savers who lend short term and mortgagors who usually borrow initially for twenty to thirty years (although the actual average duration of a mortgage is about seven years). The rate of interest on both new and existing mortgages is varied in order to bring supply and demand for funds into equilibrium. The building societies have grown from holding assets of £77 million in 1919 to £15,250 million in 1972. The first wave of expansion in building societies came in the 1930s, and coincided with a massive increase in owner-occupation. Since the Second World War there has been a continuing growth in the movement and in the 1960s this has run at well over 10 per cent per annum. This growth in assets has been used partly to increase the number of dwellings mortgaged, but also it has been required, especially in the last two or three years, to allow for the increase in the size of each mortgage as house prices have risen. Indeed in real terms there has been hardly any growth in the last year.

Although building societies are the major source of demand, finance insurance companies, banks and local authorities are also involved in providing funds. In comparison with building societies insurance companies normally mortgage relatively high quality, high priced dwellings. They attempted to expand this business in the early 1960s but lately their involvement has been declining. In 1972 insurance companies lent £145 million as against the £3,649 million lent by the building societies, while insurance companies' advances outstanding at the end of September 1972 were £1,159 million as against the building societies' £12,078 million. Banks are generally only involved in short-term loans to be used for bridging purposes. The amount that they lend each year reflects the ease or difficulty of general credit rather than any overall trends in mortgage finance. For instance in 1969, a time of credit control, total bank lending was £5 million; in 1971, a fairly normal year, they lent £90 million and in 1972, a time of enormous credit expansion, total lending was £325 million. Local authority lending for house purchase is of roughly the same magnitude as that by insurance companies: £191 million advanced in 1972 with £1,123 million worth of loans outstanding at the end of September 1972. However local authorities generally lend only to the lower end of the market so that the number of mortgages actually covered by this total is very much greater − 45,202 in 1972 as against 24,750 by the insurance companies. Generally local authorities lend only where a mortgage has already been refused by the other institutions on grounds of the purchaser's own unsuitability or because of the relatively poor quality of the dwelling. Local authorities thus act as lenders of last resort mainly for older housing.

Because the building societies have been the main intermediary in the growth of owner-occupation, they have had extremely important effects on the nature of the housing stock. They have fairly rigid rules as to when they will arrange a mortgage. When determining this they are inclined to favour traditionally-built new or nearly new houses with three or more bedrooms, garage and garden. If the dwelling to be mortgaged does not fit this specification the building society will only advance a smaller proportion of their own valuation down to as little as 60 per cent (on purpose-built flats in the provinces) in comparison with 90 per cent or 95 per cent lent on suitable houses. It can be very difficult to obtain a mortgage at all on some types of property particularly converted flats, bed-sitting-rooms and dwellings built of wood or other non-traditional materials. Partly as a result of these restrictions there have been few changes in the type or method of construction of dwellings built for owner-occupation. Completions in the private sector are predominantly houses (170,000 as against 14,500 flats in 1972), with three or more bedrooms. In 1972, for instance, 86 per cent of all new private houses had three or more bedrooms while only 65 per cent were as large as this in the public sector.

As well as to a great extent determining the type of accommodation people can buy, building societies have strict rules in relation to the mortgagee. Normally the purchaser is not allowed to borrow more than two and a half to three times his regular annual income. This income must be secure and assured into the future. A wife's income, which is automatically regarded by the building society as uncertain, usually only allows the mortgage to be increased by an amount equal to her annual income. Even this amount may be disallowed especially when credit is generally difficult. Such rules mean for instance that a young professional man can usually obtain a mortgage much more easily than a middle-aged working couple even though their family incomes are apparently exactly the same. Thus building societies in providing an enormously important intermediary service have also greatly affected the type of houses in which people live and the type of people who live in them. This rigidity is currently under attack as the proportion of owner-occupation rises and potential purchasers fall more often into the currently unacceptable categories.

The rate of the interest at which mortgage loans are made is set by the rate of interest demanded by the small saver, plus tax on this interest (levied slightly below the average individual rate), and management and administrative costs. The rate for savers is fixed so as to bring in what building societies regard as an adequate flow of funds. Generally the mortgage rate of interest has been very favourable to borrowers especially during the last few years because small savers have not expected inflation to be as rapid as it has ultimately been and have therefore accepted relatively low rates. Mortgagors also receive tax relief on the interest paid at their marginal tax rate so the real rate of interest faced by mortgagors has been very low indeed. The incentive to become an owner-occupier and to borrow as much as possible has been very great over the last few years because building societies aid individuals who would normally not easily be able to enter the capital market to borrow at a favourable rate using the dwelling that they purchase as collateral. As well as the help provided by the building societies the government increases the incentive to house purchase through interest tax relief, and other implicit subsidies.[2] These factors, in addition to the rapid rise in house prices since the war, have made owner-occupation a very profitable investment and it is to a great extent the existence of a well-developed capital market which has made this movement into home ownership possible.

Until the 1970s building societies attempted to vary the rates of interest to borrowers and lenders as rarely as possible. Further they held high liquidity ratios which have generally not been allowed to fluctuate to any great extent. The overall liquidity ratio has normally been between 16 per cent and 19 per cent although the legal minimum is only 7.5 per cent.The building societies argue that it should be held so high because a large amount of liquidity is necessary to cover the risks involved in a combination of lending long and borrowing short. However the requirement of a relatively stable liquidity ratio together with inflexible interest rates because of high costs of varying these rates has led to enormous fluctuations in the flow of funds especially as competing institutions are inclined to change their rates more often. When building society funds are relatively low a mortgage famine occurs. This helps to stabilise or even reduce house prices but at the same time slows down sales and mobility and perhaps affects housing starts because of builders' fears of being unable to sell completed dwellings. When funds are relatively easy the societies generally lend out almost on demand, often easing their lending rules relating to mortgagors and property (which they have tightened during the shortage). The expansion in funds helps to cause a buoyant housing market and so increases house prices as latent demand is enabled to become effective. Rapid movement between famine and flood has been a feature of the last few years. The enormous price increases of 1971 – 72, which were followed by a mortgage famine in 1973, were blamed mainly on building society inflexibility of behaviour and led to much political discussion on how to bring the availability of demand finance more in line with the supply of dwellings. The problems have always been there, resulting from the societies' generally conservative behaviour and their desire for growth as well as from the underlying difficulties of lending long and borrowing short. These problems have become more obvious at the present time particularly because greater than expected inflation erodes savings, engenders uncertainty about the future and requires more rapidly changing interest rates to produce a stable flow of funds. Government attempts to create more competition in the money market have also exacerbated this trend because they have led to banks and other institutions bidding up interest rates to attract funds.

Over the century building societies have been of tremendous importance in the housing market especially through their affect on tenure structure. Their existence has expanded access to the capital market for a very wide range of people, but they have also been very conservative in their attitude to house types and to mortgagors. Now they are finding it difficult to determine their role in financing demand in a situation where half the population already owns their house and where inflation is leading to the need to vary both their borrowing and lending behaviour. Continuing rapid inflation may well cause massive changes in the methods of financing house purchase and may even slow down growth of owner-occupation. In the short-term also the availability of funds to building societies and thus the quantity of mortgages they are prepared to issue has tremendously large effects on demand and possibly on supply of housing and therefore on the new housing market.

3.3 The financing of supply

Unlike many industries which self-finance, house-building finance comes mainly from outside sources particularly from the banks. The building process is suitable for this type of financing in that the value of the property as it is built acts as specific increasing collateral to the increasing loan. Further, the period of building (usually under a year) is a fairly normal one for arranging short-term overdrafts and loans. Once a particular dwelling is completed and sold the original debt is repaid and a new loan for the next house to be built is negotiated. In general this method of financing is comparatively cheap for the builder because he only pays for what he is actually borrowing at the time. However there are disadvantages especially in that the banks have control over almost all the available finance and can restrict output very considerably. Yet this is not altogether a disadvantage from the point of view of the building firm because there are often few costs of not building. House builders in Britain generally have few fixed costs, a small number of employees and little working capital. The smallest firms have alternative possibilities of income from house improvement and general repairs as do the employees of the larger firms. So firms often enter the industry when times are good and exit when they are bad. Because of these alternative possibilities and the lack of capital tied up in the industry, firms perhaps also do not have as much incentive as in many industries to obtain an even level of output. Their dependence on outside finance exacerbates these tendencies and leads to large fluctuations in the number of starts.

Some analysts[3] have argued that the level of starts is determined almost entirely by availability of funds which is in turn determined by the level of sales (which free funds to start new dwellings) and the total amount of cash that financial institutions are prepared to lend for house building. Such a model implies that availability of funds is entirely determined by the lenders mainly the banks, an extremely strong assumption. Yet most evidence does suggest that supply financing is an important variable, if not the all-important one in determining housing starts.

House-building firms usually wish to borrow large sums in relation to their own capitalisation and are 'among the less stable of businesses'.[4] Table 3.1 gives some evidence on which to base the hypothesis that house-building firms are relatively unstable. The figures are not easy to assess because bankruptcy is higher in small firms generally and house-building

Table 3.1

Bad debtors and business failures*

	Total	Building and construction	Percentage of total
1967	3,266	873	26·7
1968	2,866	703	24·5
1969	3,460	810	23·4
1970	3,689	918	24·9
1971	2,734	689	25·2
1972	2,205	666	30·2

* Notified to Trade Indemnity Co. Ltd.

Source: Trade Indemnity Co. Ltd, Press Release, 10 October 1973.

firms are on average small. The series is not of adequate length to determine any statistical relationship between credit restriction and failure but at least does not contradict the generally held belief that construction firms are insecure. It would be expected that, as a result of this actual and perceived instability, banks and other financial institutions would regard builders as poor risks. They would therefore lend a smaller quantity of credit as higher rates of interest in comparison to that which the average firm can obtain. In times of credit restraint banks have considerable incentive to cut loans to builders quickly. Not only are builders normally high risk firms but as general credit becomes more difficult to obtain they also find it more difficult to sell their product. Money is thus tied up longer and the risk of loss is higher during a squeeze. This hypothesis seems to fit what evidence there is on financing the house-building industry but cannot easily be backed with statistical analysis because there is no time series data available on bank loans to house builders rather than to the construction industry as a whole. Some analysts suggest that the situation is even worse in that the government uses the building industry as an instrument of economic policy specifically ordering loan restriction to construction when deflation is required.[5] The published directives from the Bank of England do not bear this out but they are always very general and it is normally assumed that more specific requirements on where to cut loan finance are given privately. Even if the house-building industry was not singled out we would expect it to be hard hit because of the relatively low expected yield to banks from such loans when there is an overall excess demand for credit.

Table 3.2 suggests that there might be a relationship between credit controls and the number of firms but the evidence is inadequate for four reasons: (a) the figures cover the whole construction industry; (b) movement of firms from house building into labour-only subcontracting would show up only as an internal transfer; (c) the measure of credit restriction is very crude and (d) the figures cannot be normalised for other structural changes such as the introduction of SET.

After a squeeze when credit starts to pick up again a house-building firm should be able to obtain funds, but it will not normally be able to start work again immediately because of difficulties in obtaining planning permission and the requirements of design and laying down infrastructure. Even when the firm is able to start building there are many months before the completed dwelling goes on the market. The financial constraints on supply thus produce an asymmetry. Work is slowed down or stopped through direct controls immediately there is credit restriction and later this is exacerbated through mortgage difficulties. Work starts up again

39

Table 3.2

Percentage decrease in number of firms in relation to
general credit controls

	All construction firms*	Small construction firms* 0–10 employees	General credit†
1961–62	1·7	1·9	Hard
1962–63	1·3	1·7	Easy
1963–64	1·9	2·6	Easy
1964–65	1·3	1·0	Easy
		0–13 employees	
1965–66	1·7	0·8	Hard
1966–67	1·0	0·1	Easy
1967–68	1·8	2·2	Hard
1968–69	3·6	3·2	Hard – Very hard
1969–70	3·9	3·4	Hard

Sources: * Housing and Construction Statistics, no. 2.

† C.St–J. O'Herlihy and J.E. Spencer, 1972.

when credit becomes easier but the firms have to be reassembled and the houses built – so demand becomes effective through the availability of finance long before new supply is available. It appears therefore that many of the difficulties encountered in the new housing market are the results of the specialist problems of financing a durable good which takes time to build and that these are exacerbated by the old-fashioned structure of the house-building industry.[6]

The problems of financing both supply and demand lead to a number of hypotheses about housing behaviour which can only be analysed further in relation to quantitative information. This must be left until the next section.

Notes

[1] In 1968 the ratio of average price to recorded average income on mortgaged dwellings was 2·68. By the fourth quarter of 1972 this had risen to 3·24. See *Housing and Construction Statistics*,No. 4, 4th Quarter, 1972, Table no. 38.

[2] Strictly interest tax relief is now given on all loans so is not a subsidy specifically on housing. However owner-occupiers pay no capital gains tax or tax on imputed rent and so are better treated than either renters or other capital owners.

[3] See particularly the housing model built by the London Graduate School of Business — e.g. the unpublished monograph by M. Duffy, 'A Model of U.K. Private Investment in Dwellings'.

[4] Extract from Press Release by Trade Indemmity Co. Ltd., 10 October 1973. This firm suggests that these figures are representative of about 25 per cent — 30 per cent of bankruptcies.

[5] See, for example, The Building Industry ... 1962 Onwards, A Survey by *The Builder*, 1962, p. 108:

> It is widely believed in the Building Industry that when economic restraint is necessary — for example when there is a Balance of Payments crisis — the Government uses the Building Industry as its main instrument. The Treasury is thought to exercise this control by directives to the joint stock banks (via the Bank of England) to withhold loans for capital expenditure on construction work, and there is some truth in it.
>
> Developers are financed by means of advances against architects certificates as buildings are completed, provided that the developer can produce reasonable evidence that long-term capital can be raised within a reasonable period. Such advances may be reduced at times of credit stringency when, if a Bank is short of funds for lending on overdraft, such categories as export finance would have a higher priority.

[6] The positive relationship of house-building activity to the ease of finance suggested here results in rather different behaviour than that observed in the United States. There it is suggested, in for instance Chapter 7 of M. K. Evans, *Macro Economic Activity*, Harper Row, New York, 1969, that the house-building industry is treated as a residual by the financial institutions. When demand for finance is high house building obtains little finance; when there is a general slowing down in activity

house building finds it easy to obtain credit and expands.House building is thus regarded as counter-cyclical in the United States while apparently moving closely with cycle (if a little in the lead) in Britain.

4 The Importance of Government Intervention in the Housing Market

During this century three major types of policy have been used by government to affect the housing market. These are direct controls (particularly rent control), the provision of local authority housing, and the use of taxation and subsidies specific to housing in both the private and public sectors. As a result all aspects of housing behaviour have been greatly influenced by government intervention.

4.1 Direct controls

Before 1914 central government took little direct interest in housing except to set minimum standards for both new and existing stock. In urban areas, local regulations relating to fire and general public health and affecting housing quality have been in existence since the Middle Ages, but the first important national Act., setting overall minimum standards for new buildings, was the Public Health Act of 1875. This legislation was followed by a series of model building bye-laws published by the Local Government Board in the late 1870s. Since then there have been many changes and improvements in the quality of housing required, culminating in the *Parker Morris Report* of 1961.[1] This determined physical standards for new local authority dwellings and defined the minimum square footage and amenities, including central heating, required in order to obtain a subsidy from central government. New dwellings in the private sector are not required to meet these specific standards but are controlled by local construction regulations, planning permission requirements and building society standards. The Public Health Acts cover minimum standards for existing dwellings, and define slums and overcrowding. Above slum standards central government sets targets for the removal or rehabilitation of all dwellings that do not meet structural and amenity standards. Except through the closure and demolition of slums and public health requirements which affect the worst quality dwellings government has no direct control over the standards of the existing stock and can only attempt to affect this through taxation and subsidy.

As well as direct controls on the quality of buildings central government has been involved in controls on price for most of this century. During the first World War almost no new buildings were added to the stock but at the same time households moved around a lot. As a result the housing shortage became so serious that in 1915 the first Rent Act was passed freezing the rents of lower priced unfurnished dwellings at the August 1914 level.[2] The Act was intended to be temporary but instead of being repealed it was in fact extended and modified immediately after the war. Among the modifications there were ones to allow some rent increases but at the same time medium priced rental housing was included for the first time. Partial decontrol did not come until 1921, and then only when vacant possession was obtained. After this there were minor changes until 1933 when all middle range housing was decontrolled. But at the same time any further decontrol on lower range houses was stopped as there was still a shortage of suitable housing.[3] The Ridley Commitee was set up to examine the situation and reported in 1937.[4] The Commitee suggested complete decontrol in some regions because the housing shortage seemed to have disappeared (although a minority report for the first time suggested permanent rent control). Before these recommendations could be implemented the Second World War broke out. Immediately rent control was reintroduced for all houses with rateable values of £100 or less in London, £90 in Scotland and £75 elsewhere, and rents were frozen at the 1 September 1939 level.

After the war an attempt was made to control furnished accommodation for the first time but it was ineffective. Apart from this, few changes were made in the 1939 Act until 1954 when landlords were allowed to increase rents if repairs had been made.[5] In 1957 another Rent Act was passed.[6] This aimed at gradual complete decontrol as dwellings fell vacant and immediate decontrol of houses of rateable values above £40 in Greater London and Scotland and £30 elsewhere. The Act also allowed considerable increases in rents for those dwellings still controlled. This Act was strongly criticised because there followed a massive decrease in the number of properties available for rent and there were also continuous price rises.[7]

In 1965, the Labour government who had always disliked the 1957 Act reintroduced rent control in the private sector.[8] It was in this Act that the concept of a 'fair rent' for private unfurnished tenancies was first introduced. A 'fair rent' is defined as 'the likely market rent that a dwelling could command if supply and demand for rented accommodation were broadly in balance in the area concerned.'[9] This is interpreted to mean that the rent assessment, made by the local Rent Officer (or by the Rent Assessment Commitee if there is disagreement between landlord and tenant) is not expected to take any account of shortage. The concept clearly has no economic meaning for if demand and supply are in balance then the rent is the market rent, which is not the rent intended by the Act. As all the stock is in existence at the time of assessment the economist would expect the rent to be a function of demand above the marginal cost of maintaining the property or the alternative cost if the dwelling can be used for another use this would include a shortage element. In the event the term has been interpreted as a valuer's concept based on the Rent Officer's subjective assessment of standards and amenities supplied by the accommodation and by the immediate neighbourhood. The resultant rent cannot be higher than the market rent but where it is set lower it takes no direct account of either costs of supply or quality demanded. There is no requirement that the 'fair rent' system should necessarily provide a normal return on historic capital and in general the Act gives no incentive to landlords to provide more property in the private unfurnished rental sector. On the other hand the Act does allow for increases in rent when repairs and improvements are carried out and so gives a reasonable return on new capital expenditure. After the 1965 Act the sector continued to decline although controlled rents have generally been raised from their previous levels.In 1971, for instance, an examination of a sample of previous rents and registered rents showed an average rise in Greater London of from £186 to £270 and in the rest of England and Wales from £94 to £146 per annum.

In 1972 the Conservative government introduced the Housing Finance Act. This speeded up the changeover from controlled to fair rents to bring all unfurnished private tenancies into the system by 1976. At the same time it introduced the same 'fair rent' structure to the public sector [10] and provided rent rebates or allowances for low income families in all unfurnished rental accommodation. Thus rent control, extended to 40 per cent of dwellings in Great Britain, continues in a modified and flexible form. Rents are reviewed at three-year intervals but tenants who pay the registered rent have continuing security of tenure.

The rents of private furnished accommodation are generally market rents although sitting tenants can go to the Rent Tribunal to obtain an assessed rent if they believe their rent to be unreasonable. The tribunal can give up to six months security of tenure and can extend this but there is no long-term security in the furnished sector. Housing allowances have been made available for low-income private furnished tenants since 1973.[11]

Rent control has been in force for private lower income housing except for furnished tenancies, since 1915. This continuing control has been an important, although not the only, factor in the contraction of the private rental sector from 90 per cent in 1914 to less than 20 per cent now. At the present time it seems likely that 'fair rent' controls will continue for many years. As the rate of return on such rents is not high we expect that proportion of private tenancies to dwindle rapidly as properties empty to be replaced mainly by local authority accommodation. Indeed there is now quite a strong movement especially in London to municipalise all non-luxury private rental accommodation.

Direct controls on rents have been a major factor in the private market while the lack of control on furnished tenancies has often led to the worst-off paying most because unlike all other sectors of the housing market access is only restricted by price. Central government control elsewhere in the housing market even in the provision of local authority housing has been indirect via taxation and subsidy until the Housing Finance Act of 1972 where central government took control of rents in the public sector. But these indirect controls have been immensely important in affecting the housing situation and to examine these we look first at the effects of local authority provision.

4.2 The provision of local authority housing

Although central government is only involved indirectly in its provision, the importance of public building and ownership of housing for lower income groups is very great. The actual decision and control processes are under the local authorities who have been entitled to provide housing since 1851. Few authorities used this right until after the First World War and at that time the total number of local authority dwellings available was negligible.

The first important Act concerned with the provision of low income housing was the Town and Country Planning Act of 1919. Local authorities were required to prepare plans to meet their housing 'needs' by building new dwellings with the help of a central government subsidy. At the same time the Act fixed minimum standards and allowed subsidies for private development. This Act was an attempt to increase general construction rather than particularly to create a housing sector directly under public control. All subsidies were withdrawn in 1921 but were reintroduced in a modified form in 1923 when the emphasis was placed on private building. The 1924 Housing Act was an about-turn restricting subsidies for private development to houses for rental and this was ineffective in expanding output and by 1930 building of this type had virtually stopped. The Act also reintroduced a housing subsidy to local authorities which continued until 1933when the subsidy was restricted to slum clearance and assistance in removing overcrowding. The changes were based on a general belief that there were no major shortages except in the lower income range. Between the wars, government subsidies were given on 1,332,000 local authority and 471,000 private houses. Taken together subsidies were provided for well over one third of the total number of houses built between 1919 and 1939.

In 1944 the government reintroduced general housing subsidies to local authorities. There were numerous variations in the level of the subsidy aimed both at encouraging more local authority building, as in 1946, or slowing it down, as in 1956. [12] The past variations in subsidies over the period from 1919 led to many problems for local authorities. The method of calculating the overall subsidy obtained from the central government depended upon when the existing houses were built. Generally the more dwellings the authority had already built the higher the subsidy and the less the burden on the rates of building new dwellings and inherently the easier it was to build more. Many local authorities which needed to build new housing could not obtain much subsidy under the regulations, while areas that built in the inter-war period qualified for large subsidies, while often not needing to build at all. The Housing Finance Act, 1972, made some attempt to rationalise the situation but at the same time reduced the real incentives for local authorities to build. All existing housing subsidies to local authorities are to be phased out except for the slum clearance subsidy which is still automatically provided. A Rising Cost Subsidy is payable, mainly in housing stress areas, when the costs of providing new housing rise faster than rental income. Otherwise, except for transitional subsidies, each local authority is expected to pay its housing costs out of its own rental income. Thus except in relation to new additions to stock in high cost areas local authorities must break even in housing for the first time since the War. Yet at the same time it has been recognised in theory that the private sector will disappear and the local authorities must provide all new accommodation for rental by lower income groups. [13]

Local authority housing is allocated on the basis of each council's own rules. There are some pre-requisites. First served are welfare families referred to the authority by the courts and other homeless families who are living in the borough. Next the council has an obligation to re-house in suitable accommodation all households who are made homeless by slum clearance and other demolition programmes. Finally accommodation goes to those on the waiting list. In most areas housing goes first to people from overcrowded accommodation or dwellings where basic amenities are lacking. Although anyone who has lived in the area for some time can normally join the waiting list, in large urban areas their chance of obtaining a council house will be very slim if the household does not consist of a family with children or otherwise fit one of the other categories listed above. Single persons (except old people), people without children and those who move from area to area have almost no chance of council accommodation.

The main offsetting factor to this situation is the New and Expanding Town policy which provides homes and jobs mainly for younger skilled workers. Such towns are located all over the country and roughly 10,000 new homes are built there each year. In these towns access policy tries to provide a fairly normal distribution of households by specified characteristics within each area.

A further supplement to local authority housing is provided by housing associations. [14] These became important under the Conservative government's 1961 Housing Act which set up a loan scheme to help associations both to build new dwellings and buy up older property. Most of the schemes are run jointly with the local authorities and many of the units go to people off the waiting list. Currently about ten thousand dwellings are being built each year for housing associations.

Although most of those in council accommodation are families on lower incomes many council tenants now wish to buy their own houses. Both the sale of council houses and building for sale by local authorities is legally allowed to a limited extent but it varies greatly from area to area. In general such policy matters are determined by local government but at times central government attempts to prohibit, reduce or even expand such sales. For instance in 1968 the Minister of Housing required annual sales of council houses to be reduced to no more than one half of 1 per cent of the local authority stock in any area. Council houses may not be sold to sitting tenants at less than 80 per cent of cost or valuation whichever is the higher, but as well as this subsidy generally the tenant is often able to obtain a mortgage on relatively easy terms from the local authority. The tenant thus usually gets a bargain. Table 4.1 shows the growth in such sales, a trend which was only reversed during the final years of the last Labour government.

Local authorities affect the available stock not only by new building

Table 4.1

Sale of local authority houses:* England and Wales

	Total	Pre-war	Post war	
			Built for sale	Other
1953–59	14,022			
1960	3,169	1,033	1,408	728
1963	4,131	1,180	1,299	1,652
1965	5,292	979	1,871	1,443
1968	9,979 ·	2,813	1,408	5,758
1970	6,816	2,069	585	4,162
1971	17,214	5,363	363	11,488
1972	45,878	11,666	820	33,392

* Excluding sales by New Town Development Corporations.

Sources: *Housing Statistics,* no. 9, 1968, Table 52. *Housing and Construction Statistics,* no. 4, 1972, Table 41.

and access rules but also through their active involvement in slum clearance since the middle of the last century. Local councils have power to compulsorily purchase dwellings or to designate them as unfit. The authority is then required to rehouse the occupants in suitable alternative accommodation. Subsidies are given by the central government, either, as between 1945 and 1972, for the provision of the necessary new dwellings or, as since 1972, for the purchase and clearance of the land. The removal of slums is often hampered by the shortage of available accommodation and this problem has existed at least in some regions during the whole of the century. The speed at which slum clearance has progressed fluctuates considerably, depending upon the government in power and the level of economic activity in the country. Since the Second World War the trend in clearance has been rapidly upwards but it will still take many years to remove all the existing slums. A longer discussion of the effects on overall stock can be found in Chapter 2.

4.3 Taxation and subsidy

Over the century, the government has evolved a very wide and complex range of taxes and subsidies relating both to the supply of dwellings and to the individuals living there. Through these taxes and subsidies the total available stock, its quality and tenure have been affected very considerably. We look first at subsidies to supply, other than those covered by the section on provision of local authority dwellings.

Until 1945 government subsidies to private sector supply were restricted mainly to new building. After the Second World War however there was a growing movement towards improving rather than clearing sub-standard dwellings because of the enormous numerical shortage. In accordance with this aim the government gave grants to private owner-occupiers and to public and private landlords to help with repairs and conversion. The first important measure was the 1949 Housing Act which gave local authorities power with certain restrictions to pay half the cost of conversion or improvement of sub-standard houses in the private sector. These restrictions were reduced in 1952 and again in 1954. In 1959 specified grants for the provision of the five standard amenities were introduced. [15] These were available by right to owners of property, public or private, which did not have these basic amenities. Additional discretionary grants continued to be available. The size of these grants was found not to be enough to cause landlords of controlled tenancies to take them up. To overcome this the Housing Act of 1964 made it possible for local authorities to carry out improvements and then charge the landlord. If this method is felt to be unsuitable the local authority may instead buy up the dwelling, renovate it and let it as a council house. Since then a number of changes have been made to increase the size of loans and ease the conditions attached. [16] For instance the Housing Act of 1971 gave considerably higher grants until 1974 for improvement in development and improvement areas in an attempt to try and speed up rehabilitation. The new White Paper *Better Homes the Next Priority* [17] places the emphasis on improvement of whole areas, called 'housing action areas', rather than simply individual dwelling units, and in general government policy is continuing to move away from demolition towards renovation and conversion. Such a policy is seen as being the quickest and cheapest way of bringing the quality of the housing stock up to a minimum level with as little social upheaval as possible.

There has been considerable criticism of the principles of improvement on the grounds that it can result in increased rents too high for the original tenants to pay or in the sale of the renovated property for owner-occupation when the tenants can be removed. Further, many of the grants anyway go to owner-occupiers, who obtain capital gains as a result of the improvements, and even to people who are buying second homes. Although there is no doubt that the improvement subsidies have increased the standards of the stock of dwellings, they have also reduced the available accommodation for the poor who cannot necessarily obtain local authority housing and are dependent upon the diminishing supply of private rental accommodation. The direct distributional effects may also be adverse in that subsidies sometimes give large capital gains to owners, who may well be property companies. [18]

Looking next at demand subsidies the decline of the private rental sector has also been hastened by differential taxation burdens between landlords and owner-occupiers. Landlords are treated like any other owners of capital, paying tax on income and capital gains while obtaining tax relief on the costs of provision. The tenant is also taxed on the income from which he pays the rent. The owner-occupier on the other hand pays no capital gains, no tax on the implicit rental income from his accommodation and obtains tax relief on the interest on any mortgage payments. There may also be the gain from owning an asset of increasing value which allows the owner-occupier to hedge against inflation. As a result anyone who can raise a mortgage and make a down-payment will normally get better value buying rather than renting. [19] On the supply side taxation policy and rent control together mean it can hardly by worthwhile for anyone to become a landlord in the private unfurnished rented sector except in the luxury class. Even in the furnished sector the rate of return is likely to be low compared with other investments unless standards provided are kept low and there is high density occupation. The history of taxation and subsidies and their effect on the housing market, especially in the private rental sector, are discussed very carefully by A. A. Nevitt. [20]

The Conservative government did try and increase the number of new houses available for private rental via housing associations. The 1961 Housing Act set up a loan scheme to help housing associations and this was extended in 1963. [21] Under the Housing Finance Act, 1972, those associations which provide rental accomodation were brought within the 'fair rent' and rent allowance schemes. Although privately owned in other ways they are financed and run in much the same way as council houses. The Conservative government saw these associations as very important and flexible components of the housing stock but there seems little likelihood that a really significant number of houses will be provided in this way.

The Housing Finance Act (1972), by introducing 'fair rents' which are generally higher than those which obtained before the Act reduced the implicit subsidy to tenants in the local authority and private unfurnished sectors from rent set below market rent. This change increased the incentive to move into owner-occupation at least for higher income tenants. The removal of the 'subsidy' was offset for lower income tenants by the implementation of a housing rebate or allowance scheme payable to individual tenants. The way the rebate or allowance is determined takes account of the rent payable, the family income and the number of people in the household and means that low income families obtain a quite considerable subsidy towards their housing costs. This direct subsidy to tenants applies to all qualifying households in both public and private sectors although the requirements for eligibility are stricter in the private furnished sector.

Owner-occupiers have historically been well treated by central government. Tax relief on mortgage interest derived originally from the first income tax legislation of 1798.[22] Even when, in 1969, the Labour government abolished tax relief on interest generally it gave specific exemption to the interest paid on loans for the acquisition or improvement of property. Additional aid was given to owner-occupiers when Schedule 'A' Tax was abolished in 1963. This was a tax on the implicit rental income from house ownership against which maintenance costs could be offset. Before 1963 housing was treated like any other investment except that income was taxed annually instead of on sale.By abolishing Schedule 'A' the relative gain from owning rather than renting was increased in line with general policies to extend home ownership. Government has tried to help further by assisting people who would not normally be eligible for a mortgage and aiding the purchase of older accommodation not easily mortgageable. As one way of doing this the Guarantee Scheme was brought in in 1958 to help building societies lend up to 95 per cent of the purchase price on relatively low quality housing. Local authority mortgages are also given to individuals who cannot obtain one from a building society and on property which does not meet building society standards. The Housing (Financial Provisions) Act 1958, and later legislation allowed the local authorities to lend up to 100 per cent of the purchase price.

In 1967 the Labour government brought in an option mortgage scheme by which those who have low tax liabilities, and therefore cannot gain maximum tax relief, are able to exchange this relief for a subsidy which reduces the mortgage rate of interest they must pay. The mortgage is then guaranteed by the central government. Owner-occupation has as a result of this and other measures become possible for a far larger proportion of the population since the war.

The use of these three types of measure, direct control, taxation and subsidy of individuals and aids to supply, has meant that government policy has been the most important factor in a near-complete revolution of the distribution of tenure from private rental to owner-occupation and local authority rental. Government has also had a considerable influence on the standard of housing provided and has aimed to house everyone to a minimum standard considerably higher than that which a large percentage of the population would effectively demand without aid. Much of this has been done by piecemeal legislation and even now there is no coherent general housing policy covering all aspects of the market.

Conclusion to Part I

In this introductory section there has been no attempt to cover all aspects of the housing situation. We have concentrated mainly on factors relevant to the later quantitative work: the economic factors which have determined demand and supply of new housing in the past.

One of the most relevant variables in a market for durable goods, where new building only accounts for a maximum of 2 per cent of the total available, must be the existing stock. We have found that the rate of addition to the existing stock has increased throughout most of the century. Even so, there has rarely been enough housing to meet social needs throughout the country although the situation is better in some regions than others. The standards and amenities available in a large proportion of existing dwellings are below government determined standards. Yet there is little evidence to suggest that effective demand would be high enough for these standards to be demanded without subsidy. Much new housing is therefore forthcoming as a result of government policies to subsidise local authority supply, slum clearance and improvements, tenants of all types, and owner-occupiers.

Probably the most important trend this century, other than the simple increase in the numbers of dwellings available, has been the change in tenure structure. From building predominantly for private rental market at the beginning of the century the situation has moved to one where almost all new building is for owner-occupation or for local authority tenancies. The most important variables in determining tenure appear to be changes in the ease of finance, government policies particularly relating to taxation and subsidy and the continuing inflation which makes housing a good asset to hold. The growth of building societies has made it possible for people to own their own homes while government subsidies and generally rising prices have meant that owner-occupation is more worthwhile than renting. On the other hand government policies have helped the decline in the private rental sector through rent control, other legislation and through taxation policies. For those who cannot afford to buy housing of reasonable standard, or in some cases have not wished to do so, the only alternative is more and more local authority rental housing.This is normally not immediately available except for welfare cases. So lower income, non-problem, families, especially new households are likely to have the choice of buying, for which they may not have access to capital, paying uncontrolled rents for furnished tenancies or living with another family. In the future the range of choice may well become simply either owner-occupation or renting from the local authority.

While examining changes in the housing situation over the century we have suggested that certain economic factors are particularly relevant in analysing the demand and supply of new housing. We expect demand to be affected by income and the ability to pay as well as by the availability and cost of financing a mortgage. Changes in the rate of inflation will also affect the demand for housing as an asset. Government policies are important not only directly through controls but also via taxes and subsidies and through their indirect effects on many of the other variables. Finally the existing stock, and its standards in relation to the number of households at any given time will have a very great effect on demand for new housing.

On the supply side the structure of the construction industry which is made up of many small firms, means that building is subject to wide fluctuations when general economic factors change. The main variables affecting new supply are likely to be profits based on the costs of construction relative to the selling price, and the availability of finance. Within the total new housing market relative profitability affects whether builders supply to the private or to the public sector, whether they build new houses or do repairs and maintenance on existing dwellings, or even whether they move into non-house-building construction. Again we expect the government to affect all these variables directly and indirectly, in particular perhaps through control of finance and through the supply of land made available for housing.

So far we have only looked at the history of these factors during this century. Such a description is valuable because it brings out the critical relationships, but it is only a preliminary to the attempt to construct quantitative models. It is to this that we now turn. The aim is to test whether some of the relationships hypothesised in this section do exist in the new housing market. If so we must then examine different specifications of the general relationships to obtain closer understanding of the

54

underlying form of this market. If an adequate structure is obtained it will be possible to examine the size of the parameters and thus the quantitative effect of each of the independent variables on the demand and supply of new housing.

Notes

[1] *Homes for Today and Tomorrow,* Report of Subcommittee of the Central Housing Advisory Committee for the Ministry of Housing and Local Government, HMSO, London 1961.

[2] The Increase of Rent and Mortgage Interest (War Restrictions) Act, 1915.

[3] Lower range housing was then defined as below £20 rateable value in London, £26.10s.0d in Scotland and £13 elsewhere.

[4] *Report of the Interdepartmental Committee on the Rent Restriction Acts* (the Ridley Committee), Cmnd 5621, HMSO, London 1937.

[5] There was a large number of white papers published just after the war which attempted to explain the housing situation. The most important of these were *Rents − Report of the Interdepartmental Committee on Rent Control,* Cmnd 6621, HMSO, 1945, and a report by the Ministry of Health, *Rent Control in England and Wales,* C133, HMSO, 1946. In the early 1950s there was an attempt to obtain the necessary information on which to base a change in policy, and this led to important reports by the Ministry of Housing and Local Government: *Housing − the Next Step*, Cmnd. 8996, 1953, and *Rent Control Statistical Information*, Cmnd. 17, 1955.

[6] The Rent Act, 1957.

[7] The results of the 1957 Act were analysed in a report by P.G. Gray and E. Parr for the Ministry of Housing and Local Government: *Some Effects of the 1957 Rent Act*, Cmnd 1246, HMSO, 1960.

[8] The Rent Act, 1965.

[9] Report of the Department of the Environment: *Fair Deal for Housing.* Cmnd 4728, HMSO, 1971, para. 23.

[10] Before 1971 each local authority had had control over the methods of determining individual rents as long as the resulting accounts were satisfactory. There were wide variations in the methods used and in the rents charged but the most usual system was to base rents on historic costs including subsidy often with an element of 'pooling' i.e. cross-subsidised from older to newer property.

[11] Under the Furnished Lettings (Rent Allowances) Act, 1973.

[12] For a discussion of post-war developments in housing policy and the role of local authorities see J.B. Cullingworth, 1966. For a study of pre-war government policy see M.E.A. Bowley, *Housing and the State.* Allen & Unwin, London 1945.

[13] A statement of the statutory duties of housing authorities can be found in Chapter 2 of the National Board for Prices and Incomes, *Increases in Rents of Local Authority Housing,* Report no. 62, Cmnd 3604, HMSO, 1968.

[14] Housing associations are non-profit bodies which provide housing both for owner-occupation by the associations' members and for rental mainly for lower income groups (especially old people).

[15] These amenities are (a) internal WC; (b) hot and cold water; (c) fixed bath; (d) basin; (e) ventilated food cupboard.

[16] See e.g., Ministry of Housing and Local Government *Old Houses into New Homes* Cmnd 3602, HMSO, 1968.

[17] Department of the Environment; *Better Homes the Next Priority* Cmnd 5339, HMSO, 1973.

[18] The white paper puts forward a number of proposals to reduce the gains to owners. No grants will be given for second homes and anyone selling rental property within seven years must return the grant with interest.

[19] In a perfect market of course the rates of return in the rental and owner-occupied markets would equate, the only losers being those who did not predict the tax, inflation and other (mainly rent control) changes. However the finance market for housing is extremely imperfect. Even if the market were perfect the tax structure would imply a reduced proportion of the total stock in the private rental sector in comparison to a no tax position.

[20] See A.A. Nevitt, *Housing, Taxation and Subsidy* Nelson, London 1966.

[21] Co-ownership schemes which lead ultimately to owner-occupation were also helped via option mortgage subsidies backed by government guarantee.

[22] See Department of the Environment: *Fair Deal for Housing*, Cmnd 4728, HMSO, 1971, para. 7.

PART II

A Model of the New Housing Market

5 Earlier Work

5.1 Introduction

In this section we examine possible econometric models which can be used to describe the new private housing market. Before choosing the structures to test we look first at the evidence available from earlier theoretical and empirical work on housing relating to both the United Kingdom and the United States.

Empirical work has been concentrated on two main areas relating to housing at the national level. Firstly there have been attempts to build models of the whole economy which include housing equations explaining expenditure, investment and the financing of housing demand and supply. These are interested only in housing as an important part of GNP. Secondly there have been a number of attempts to build models of the housing sector (usually only of new construction) which take the variables relating to the rest of the economy as exogenously determined. These wish to explain the behaviour of the housing market for its own sake. We will examine these two types of models and the results relevant to our own hypotheses in some detail but first we assess the relevance of theoretical work on housing particularly in relation to owner-occupation.

There has not been much theoretical work relating to housing specifically. In general it has been seen simply as an example of a necessary consumer good — an extreme oversimplification as there are a number of factors which make housing different from other goods. These include:

1   Housing is a durable good providing both necessary and luxury consumption services as well as having an asset value to the owner.

2   Housing is a heterogenous product consisting of many different qualities and quantities of housing service. Moreover once a house has been built it cannot be moved to another area. The market may easily be in excess demand in one area and in excess supply in another and suppliers can do little about it. The market is inherently imperfect, but because purchasers may be prepared to trade-off different attributes within houses when choosing, one house cannot easily be compared with another and it is difficult to assess the nature and extent of these imperfections.

3   Housing is a large part of a family's budget, on average about 15 per cent of household expenditure and probably the largest single purchase that is made during a lifetime. The price of a house is usually about three or more times the annual income of the purchaser. In the majority of cases it is necessary for the household to borrow money on the capital market to finance the purchase. Access to capital is generally dependent upon income, health and security and therefore different individuals in apparently similar circumstances have different costs of borrowing.

4   The supply of housing cannot be changed very rapidly because new building is such a small proportion of existing stock. It is also difficult to vary the existing housing stock to meet changes in demand, although conversion and improvements may be used to supplement new building.

5   There are lags in reaction both in demand and supply. On the supply side there is a time lag between the decision to produce and the actual supply of new dwellings because of the time taken to design and build new houses. On the demand side reaction to changes in income, price, credit, etc. is likely to be slow because the decision to move is taken irregularly and costs of movement are high.

6   As we have discussed in detail in section one the government intervenes in the housing market in all its aspects through both demand and supply. They are involved directly by the provision of local authority housing and indirectly through legislation on pricing, standards, zoning, etc. and via taxation and subsidy. All these have important effects on the housing market and any changes should be built into any empirical model of the housing market. This however is a policy of perfection and with the current state of data availability is quite impossible.

5.2   Theoretical work

Most theoretical analyses do not take the problems mentioned above into account to any great extent. Often work concentrates on a single theoretical problem where housing can be used as an example. The most obvious case of this is the analysis of price controls where rent control is one of the most long-standing instances of such government intervention. Mostly these discussions take little account of the special circumstances of the housing market but look at the problem in general terms. An example is the analysis found in Ryan.[1] A more sophisticated model is analysed by

Gould and Henry.[2] This uses rent control of housing as an example of a price control and shows that under the normal assumptions it is not possible to predict whether price will rise or fall in a related market as a result of price in the controlled market being held below equilibrium. It requires, however, only the single extra assumption of exclusive markets (i.e. that no consumer enters both the rent controlled market and the free market) to show that the price in the related market will go up as a result of increased demand in the controlled market.[3] The main use of their article is not to explain the housing market but to show that predictions, even in simple situations of this nature, are dependent upon very restrictive assumptions. As soon as reactions in supply are postulated in addition to changes in demand it is impossible to obtain any predictions as to the effect on quantity or price in related markets. Such work suggests that although comparative statistics may bring problems to light they are not normally able to make predictions which are testable. Such analysis is not a very fruitful area of research at the present time.

Another area of theoretical analysis which is perhaps more applicable to the US market than to Britain is that of filtering. The hypothesis suggests that there is no need to build lower income housing. If all new supply is of good quality houses for high income groups, then dwellings vacated by the buyers of new houses will filter down to the next income level and in turn their houses will filter further. The principle is explained in detail by Grigsby[4] and considerable work has been done in extending the model although little empirical testing has been attempted.[5] This type of analysis is based on assumptions which are not fully reflected in the UK market. The basic assumption required for the prediction is that the housing market is relatively free and that the government only intervenes indirectly. The discussions also usually assume that equilibrium exists in the short-run. If there is a situation of shortage alleviated by government building at the lower income level the analysis becomes less relevant. However, the general approach is an attempt to relate the new and existing housing markets and may be of use in later analyses once we have obtained an adequate explanation of the new housing market.[6]

The other theoretical area where housing has been seen as an integral part of the problem is the theory of business cycles. It has been argued that historically there are long cycles in investment in particular in residential construction. This has been discussed in considerable detail by Parry Lewis[7] in this country and by Duesenberry, Hansen and Abromovitz[8] in the United States. The cycle was thought to be of about twenty years' duration and to be the result of changes in demographic and other exogenous factors such as war. They argue that these exogenous 'shocks' have effects

61

on the economy as a whole which are magnified in the housing market because of the durability and necessity of the good. The post-war housing market does not really appear to fit the long-cycle hypothesis and at least in the United States new theories of investment in the residential construction market have been developed based more on supply than demand factors.[9] Guttentag[10] has tested a theory which suggests that credit for home builders and buyers is a residual from the point of view of financiers. If total credit available remains fairly constant over the business cycle residential construction will be essentially counter-cyclical. This does appear to fit the US data. Little work has been done on this aspect of housing in the UK. The most interesting approach is that by Vipond[11] which examined the relationship between house-building activity and the business cycle using general statistical observations rather than by building a full model. She concludes that private housebuilding activity is cyclical and depends mainly on income growth, building costs and the availability of credit. Public investment in dwellings shows more stable behaviour but is also certainly not countercyclical. In order to test the theory adequately a model of the whole investment sector of the national economy with housing investment treated separately, would be required, if not a complete model of the economy. Any results would add considerably to our knowledge of new housing as a component of investment and its relation to the financial sector but would require a very sophisticated model of the housing market.

This last type of theoretical analysis is very strongly related to other methods of examining the housing market, in particular econometric models of the whole economy and of the housing sector. We next discuss work which has been published in these areas.

5.3   Empirical analyses

There have been a large number of attempts to build models of the US national economy which explain short-term fluctuations in output. Most of these include housing sectors of more or less sophistication. There have also been a number of models which attempt to explain only the housing sector.

Empirical work done before 1960 is discussed in an article by Grebler and Maisel which attempted to review and compare all the models of residential construction available at the time.[12] They concluded that although certain authors had identified important variables, particularly those relating to credit, there had been no real success in building a full predictive model for either the short or long term. In 1971 Fromm repeated the exercise for the most important models then in use. [13] He compares eight national economy and three housing sector models. All concentrate on short-term phenomena usually relegating long-term variables such as population and household formation to a time-trend or to a single-trend style variable such as income or the number of marriages. All the models specify market supply and demand relationships and usually attempt to take account of any disequilibrium effects through the addition of constraint variables such as credit availability or by specifically introducing variations in vacancy rates. Fromm's main complaint is that most analyses take ad hoc sets of variables which appear to explain supply, demand and disequilibrium in practice without basing this empirical work fully in economic theory. He argues that mis-specification occurs because of the problems of autocorrelation in time-series estimation and because simple equations cannot adequately reflect the complexity of administrative and legal constraints or imperfections in the housing and capital markets. Most of the models concentrate on demand relationships and the effects of finance. Little notice is taken of costs of labour and construction and supply specifications are generally primitive. Most of the models are very aggregated taking little account of different types of dwelling, variation in government subsidies and regional differences. Finally even in 1971 most analyses were done using ordinary least-squares with no attempt to remove the biases involved from attempting to estimate a full model in this way or the autocorrelation which is such a major difficulty in time-series analyses of this type of market.

Fromm's conclusion is that all the models that were available in 1971 were unsatisfactory and, without exception, unreliable for forecasting purposes. Some of the difficulties cannot be overcome without building enormously complex models for which the data does not exist. Others could be reduced by using better econometric techniques and by further examination of the underlying economic theories particularly those relating to durable goods. Although Fromm's discussion is extremely critical he concludes that the work, however imperfect, is worthwhile and adds to our knowledge of the housing market. His final analysis of the current situation is that 'with continued progress in formulation of hypotheses and better data, it is feasible to produce models that have greater predictive ability and can validly be used for structural analysis and policy simulation purposes'. [14]

Since 1971 some further work has been done, especially on the FRB-MIT-PENN model, but no breakthrough has yet occurred in terms of either predictive or simulation ability. In 1973 Arcelus and Meltzer reported on their model. [15] This is a good example of the current concentration on the effects of costs and availability of credit on housing. They attempt to test the hypothesis that it is restriction on the quantity of credit available that limits housing production. They argue that an alternative hypothesis is that rising interest rates lead to postponement of purchases of durable goods and these two predictions lead to very different policy implications. Their three equation model upholds the second, unconventional, view and finds that the principal determinants of housing demand are relative prices, interest rates, wealth and income. The policy implication is that simply expanding credit availability will have little effect on the housing market and what is required for expansion is stable, inflation-free growth. Although the data and estimation procedures suffer from many of the difficulties discussed by Fromm there is here a clear attempt to base the work on accepted theory and it can be regarded as a blow against ad hocery and mythology.

Similar attempts to build models of the housing sector can be found in other countries. In particular Smith has built a model of the Canadian housing sector. [16] However this work suffered from many of the faults of the American models, in particular it was unable to predict supply or demand efficiently outside its estimation period and suffered greatly from autocorrelation bias.

There has also been considerable work done on the mechanisms of the overall housing market. This work has concentrated on the analyses of the response of housing demand and supply to changes in incomes, prices, subsidies, etc. Most of the published work analyses cross-section data. The most fully-analysed area is that of income elasticities of demand. Work relating to demand published before 1970 is summarised by de Leeuw. [17] He concludes that once allowance is made for the differences in data, biases introduced by using expenditure rather than market value and other differences in specification, the income elasticity of demand for renters can be regarded as about unity while that for owner-occupiers is probably a little higher. Less work has been done on prices although de Leeuw discusses some results. Muth also looks at his own and earlier evidence and suggests that the price elasticity of demand is considerably less than unity. [18] This type of work is important to our current analysis in that it provides general information about the likely magnitude of certain coefficients.

Apart from models of residential construction within national models more and more work in the USA is now concentrating on residential location models. Except to the extent that income, price and other elasticities are necessary inputs into these models this strand of research is not relevant to our discussion and is therefore not assessed here.

In the UK there have been fewer attempts to build models of the whole economy although a number are now being developed. In the main they are very general and have little to say specific to housing. Indeed the first published model by Klein et al did not even take separate account of the housing sector but simply included it in general investment. [19]

The econometrics division of the London Graduate School of Business has built a quarterly model of the UK economy which includes a private residential construction sector. This follows American work very closely but is not specifically interested in analysing demand as such, concentrating on estimating a reduced form which determines starts. The structure is almost entirely based on financial variables including the mortgage rate, the bank rate, the net flow of funds, advances to purchasers of all types and bank advances to builders. The model suggests that credit constraints on purchasers and builders rather than real demand and supply variables determine starts. Few results have so far been reported and there are major data deficiencies. [20]

Some work has also been done on income and price elasticities. This has mainly been undertaken at the Department of the Environment using data made available by the building societies. Cross-section estimates suggest an income elasticity well below unity perhaps as low as 0·65.[21] The results also show that there are large variations in these estimates between age and income groups and between regions. The nature of the data and the estimation methods used probably bias the measure downwards. Indeed Nicholson argues that, for forecasting purposes, an estimate of unity especially when it takes account of the likely continued movement into owner-occupation, would not give very biased results. [22]

Work on forecasting demand in the medium term has also been done at the Department of the Environment under Holmans. [23] This uses estimates of the relationships between household formation and the independent variables and the demand for housing. Some of these relationships are based on tested econometric estimates but many are based on general qualitative observation. Forecasts are attempted for the next decade and more generally to the end of the century.

Finally in the UK there have been a number of attempts to build models of building society behaviour and its relationship to housing activity. The only one so far published is that by Spencer and O'Herlihy.[24] This concentrates on the financial aspects of housing and will be discussed in more detail when we formulate our own model of private construction to be tested.

5.4   The aims and limitations of the model

It is clear from the discussion of available work that any model, even of such a narrowly determined area as the new housing market, is unlikely to be more than a pilot study. If the results in the United States are only just beginning to be worthwhile after nearly twenty years of work it is improbable that any early study in Britain will produce much more than an idea of the general structure of the market with perhaps some estimates of the possible range of income and price elasticities. It is important to concentrate on clearly specifying these and other variables, such as the financial variables, likely to be of consequence, but we should also make clear that the results can only be very limited.

In 1952 Carter and Roy[25] examined the extent to which data was available in the UK to form a basis for assessing government policy. Their aim in relation to the housing sector was to discover the required size of the housing programme to meet housing *need*.[26] They wrote:

> we shall start by requiring whether the existing statistics enable us to assess the size of the housing shortage or the capacity of the building industry to build new houses. We shall find that they do not; the function of statistics in the field of policy is to provide background information, helpful but incomplete, and to throw some light on the implications of possible changes or the results of changes which have been made.

The availability of data hardly changed in the next ten years. There were two national sample surveys by the Government Social Survey examining both the quality of existing housing and households' requirements concerning housing at the date of the surveys.[27] The *Milner Holland Report*[28] gave some useful information about the housing stock in Greater London while much later the *Francis Report*[29] examined the situation in the private rental sector. Accurate information on prices, costs, especially land costs, proportion of income spent on housing and other important variables is still sparse. The main data available after the war was the number of houses started, under construction and completed by the public and private sectors published in the *Housing Returns for England and Wales, Scotland and Northern Ireland.*[30] Apart from these there were very few official time series data. The Co-operative Building Society, now the Nationwide, published information about the prices of the houses they mortgaged but there was hardly any other available information on prices.

The great change in availability of housing statistics occurred in 1966 when *Housing Statistics*[31] was published for the first time. Since then this publication has provided much necessary information on construction, improvement and demolition, costs and prices, but it had to start from such a poor base that it will take many years before the data desired by a housing economist will be available in adequate time-series form. One useful aspect of any pilot study such as this one is to point out where there is a need for data and to suggest possible ways of overcoming information problems.

As the lack of time-series data in many areas cannot be made good for many years it might be better to attempt a cross-section study. In theory this could be done using data relating to standard regions or even smaller areas. Cross-section models are useful because they can take account of the local nature of a good which once built is locationally specific. It is also a more theoretically acceptable way of obtaining income and price elasticities and would make the results compatible with those of Margaret Reid and others for the USA[32], for time-series estimates will be biased by the problem of lagged reactions. Unhappily, data, although improving as a result of the publication of *Abstract of Regional Statistics*[33] as well as *Housing Statistics*, are still unavailable for some very important variables. There is, for instance, no acceptable income variable. The Inland Revenue surveys income by region every five years but attributes income to the place it is earned rather than to the place of residence.[34] It is the consumption point which is important in determining housing expenditure. The *Family Expenditure Survey*[35] gives survey estimates of income annually but they are difficult to compare with other data, particularly because income refers to a single week and non-response varies greatly between income groups and regions. There is some information on regional prices but almost none on costs, especially land costs which are enormously variable between areas. Where such data exist the regions available are often not compatible with standard regions. So although cross-section analysis is a fruitful area for future research much of what is required is the collection of basic data rather than the construction of complex models. The difficulties involved in time-series models are enormous but less than those entailed in cross-section work at the present time.

For the reasons set out above, our aim will be to build a quantitative time-series model of the British new housing market. We now look at the nature of the questions we hope to answer through the model.

Firstly, we cannot expect to show the importance of long-run determinants of housing demand and supply such as changes in household formation and changes in building techniques because we are building a quarterly model for a period of only about fifteen years. [36] The main emphasis will therefore be on short-term determinants of new housing demand and supply.

Most economists who have worked on the housing market are agreed that finance is extremely influential. [37] It is hoped to show the effects of availability and cost of finance on the supply side by including these as separate variables in the cost structure. On the demand side costs of finance affect the price. Most people who buy houses do not buy them outright and the price to them is not simply the purchase price but that plus mortgage financing costs. [38] We will attempt to specify the price variable so that this consideration is taken into account. Also because of the building societies' rules concerning the ratio of income to monthly repayments, income is a material variable both in that it directly affects demand and in relation to the credit and price variables. We will hope to obtain reasonable estimates of the effects of price and incomes on demand using these specifications.

Another important variable which must be included in some way is the effect of inflation. [39] We intend to include some variable for inflation in the model not only because of the effect inflation has on the individual's ability to pay but also because it affects expectations relating to a person's decision to buy or rent. Moreover, if he buys, the type of house will depend partly on his estimate of the future worth of the asset and the extent to which the house can be used as a hedge against inflation. For all these reasons changes in inflation may well be influential and must be carefully and separately specified in order to show up these different influences on demand.

One aspect of housing behaviour which differs very greatly between the USA and the UK is the extent of government involvement. Because of this American models may well be unsuitable in relation to the analysis of housing in this country. In the USA the government enters the housing market mainly via the financial sector. [40] It attempts to help the individual to buy his house by aiding credit facilities. In the last few years the FHA has attempted to provide middle income housing in larger amounts in some cities [41] but generally the impact of the government has been quite small and can be adequately introduced into a model of the housing sector via credit variables and by dummies to reflect major changes in legislation. [42] In the UK this method of specification is unlikely to be adequate. The government is involved in the housing market not only through its effects on finance but also because it supplies indirectly between one third and one half of all new dwellings. In this way the government affects builders' behaviour and the costs of building in both the public and private sectors. The provision of local authority housing also affects demand for all types of housing so government policy pervades all parts of the new housing market (as it does in the total housing sector). The tremendous importance of government should be included in the model in some way even though we are concentrating specifically on the private sector which is directly affected only by finance.

In any model of the housing market we should take account of the lags involved in the process of building. Considerable work has been done on this problem for investment generally[43] because the lag between the decision to invest and capital actually coming into use is extremely important to the theory of business cycles and growth. In the housing sector the problem has been recognised but has not been examined closely. Even in the USA many models have demand and supply variables so mixed that there is really only a reduced form and the proper specification of the time lag is not possible. The difficulty was examined by Sherman Maisel in the Brookings model, [44] but there is room for considerably more research in this area. In the model we will attempt to use some of the lag structures suggested in the literature on investment especially those put forward by Koyck and Jorgenson.[45]

Finally another problem which is perhaps more important in this country than in the USA: the possibility that the housing market is not in equilibrium. In the USA the lack of government interference, the mobility of the population [46] and many other factors mean that for most purposes, as long as slow reaction to changes in independent variables is built into the specification, an equilibrium model is adequate. In the UK government control means that there may well not be equilibrium in some markets (particularly the unfurnished and the local authority sectors)[47] and the many financial and administrative constraints could mean there is no equilibrium even in the free sectors. Moreover low mobility makes specification of the lags towards equilibrium extremely difficult. The housing market is slow to adjust on the demand side because very few people are in the market at any given time although many may be dissatisfied with their dwellings because of transactions and information costs. On the supply side the slow building processes and the durability of the good means that the nature of desired supply will rarely be equal to actual supply. These problems are probably less acute in the new private housing market where most of the adjustment takes place but should be borne in mind.

In this chapter we have taken a rather cursory look at past economic research on housing and the modifications that it is intended to make in this model. All researchers involved in examining the housing market are dissatisfied by their results mainly because of the complex economic environment in which housing decisions take place. It is not expected that all of these problems can be overcome in the model we attempt to test here but we do hope to set up a viable quantitative model of the new private housing market.

Notes

[1] See W. J. L. Ryan, *Price Theory*, 2nd ed., Macmillan & Co. Ltd, London 1960, pp. 116–19, and E. H. Phelps-Brown and J. Wiseman, *A Course in Applied Economics*, 2nd ed., Pitman, London 1965, chap. 7, which uses much the same type of analysis.

[2] J. R. Gould and S. G. B. Henry, 'The Effects of Price Control in a Related Market', *Economica*, vol. XXXIV, no. 133, 1967.

[3] A different approach to the problem of related markets in housing can be found in I. Stahl, 'Some Aspects of the Mixed Housing Market' in A. A. Nevitt (ed.), *The Economic Problems of Housing*, International Economic Association Conference 1965, Macmillan, London 1967. The article is mainly descriptive pointing out how housing differs from other markets.

[4] W. G. Grigsby, *Housing Markets and Public Policy*, University of Pennsylvania Press, Philadelphia, 1963.

[5] See L. H. Klassner, 'Some Theoretical Considerations for the Structure of the Housing Market' in *University of California: Essays in Urban Land Economics*, Los Angeles 1966, which sets out a mathematical model showing the effects of changes in population, income and depreciation. He comes to the conclusion that equilibrium in the higher income bracket housing will inevitably result in excess supply at the lower rental level.

[6] The GLC has been carrying out a long-term project analysing the behaviour of chains of movers in order to analyse the filtering process in London. Results are not yet available.

[7] J. Parry-Lewis, 1965. This is very much a descriptive historical account of long cycles since the eighteenth century.

[8] J. S. Duesenberry, *Business Cycles and Economic Growth*, McGraw-Hill, New York, 1968, pp. 158–64. A. H. Hansen, *Business Cycles and National Income*, Norton, New York, 1951, chap. 3. M. Abromovitz, *Evidence of Long Swings in Aggregate Construction since the Civil War*, Princeton University Press, Princeton 1964.

[9] A survey of the current theories of investment in residential construction can be found in M. K. Evans, *Macro-economic Activity*, Harper Row, New York, 1969, chap. 7.

70

[10] J. M. Guttentag, 'The Short Cycle in Residential Construction', *American Economic Review*, vol. 51, no. 3, 1961, p. 292.

[11] M. J. Vipond, 'Fluctuations in Private Housebuilding in Great Britain 1950–66', *Scottish Journal of Political Economy*, vol. XVI, no. 2, 1969.

[12] See L. Grebler and S. J. Maisel, 'Determinants of Residential Construction: A Review of Present Knowledge' in *Commission Money and Credit 'Impacts of Monetary Policy'*, Prentice Hall, New Jersey, 1963.

[13] G. Fromm, 'Econometric Models of the Residential Construction Sector: A Comparison', paper presented at the Housing Model Conference for Federal Home Loan Bank Board, Washington DC 1971.

[14] G. Fromm, op. cit., p. 12.

[15] F. Arcelus and A. H. Meltzer, 'The Market for Housing and Housing Services', *Journal of Money, Credit and Banking*, vol. V, no. I, Part I, 1973.

[16] L. B. Smith, 'A Model of the Canadian Housing and Mortgage Markets', *Journal of Political Economy*, vol. 77, no. 5, 1969.

[17] F. de Leeuw, 'The Demand for Housing: A Review of Cross-Section Evidence', *The Review of Economics and Statistics*, vol. LIII, no. 1, 1971.

[18] R. Muth, 'The Demand for Non-Farm Housing', in A. C. Harberger (ed.) *The Demand for Durable Goods*, University of Chicago Press, Chicago 1960.

[19] L. R. Klein, R. J. Ball, J. A. Hazelwood and P. Vandome, *An Econometric Model of the UK*, Blackwell, Oxford, 1961.

[20] The model is discussed in R. J. Ball and T. Burns, 'The Prospects of Faster Growth in Britain', *National Westminster Bank Review*, November 1968. Further discussion papers are available from the Business School.

[21] I. C. R. Byatt, A. E. Holmans and D. Laidler, 'Income and the Demand for Housing: Some Evidence for Great Britain' in M. Parkin (ed.) Association of University Teachers in Economics Conference, Aberystwyth 1972, *Essays in Modern Economics*, Weidenfeld and Nicholson, London, 1973.

[22] Discussion by R. J. Nicholson in M. Parkin (ed.), op. cit., pp. 85–8.

[23] A. E. Holmans, 'A Forecast of the Effective Demand for Housing in Great Britain in the 1970s', *Social Trends*, no. 1, Central Statistical Office, London, 1970.

[24] C. St J. O'Herlihy, and J. E. Spencer, 'Building Societies' Behaviour 1955–70', *National Institute Economic Review*, no. 61, 1972.

[25] C. F. Carter and A. D. Roy, *British Economic Statistics – A Report*, Cambridge University Press, Cambridge 1952.

[26] They were also one of the first to discuss the difference between 'need' and demand (and to suggest that total demand was increased by

rent control, under-occupation and subsidies to the local authority sector). This distinction has become very important in the economic analysis of public policy, as most planners and politicians analyse housing problems in terms of 'need' without respect to the ability or desire to pay.

[27] UK Social Survey SS319, *The Housing Situation in 1960,* report by P. G. Gray and R. Russell, HMSO, London, 1962. UK Social Survey SS372, *The Housing Situation in England and Wales in 1964*, Report by Myra Woolf, HMSO, London, 1967.

[28] UK Ministry of Housing and Local Government *Report of the Committee on Housing in Greater London.* The *Milner Holland Report.* Cmnd 2605, HMSO, London, 1965.

[29] UK Department of the Environment. *Report of the Committee on the Rent Acts.* The *Francis Report*, Cmnd 4609, HMSO, London, 1971.

[30] UK Ministry of Housing and Local Government. *Housing Returns for England and Wales, Scotland and Northern Ireland*, HMSO, London, Monthly.

[31] UK Ministry of Housing and Local Government, the Welsh Office *Housing Statistics*, HMSO, London, Quarterly. In 1972 its name was changed to *Housing and Construction Statistics* published quarterly by the Department of the Environment and the Welsh Office.

[32] M.G. Reid, *Housing and Income,* University of Chicago Press, Chicago, 1962. See also the works by R. Muth and Tong Hun Lee mentioned earlier in the chapter.

[33] *Abstract of Regional Statistics* published annually since 1966 for the Central Statistical Office, HMSO, London.

[34] This can be found every five years in UK Commissioners of Inland Revenue *Annual Reports*, HMSO, London.

[35] UK Department of Trade and Industry, *Family Expenditure Survey*, HMSO, London, Annually.

[36] A discussion of long-run determinants and the extent to which short- and long-run determinants have been intermixed in model building can be found in M. K. Evans, *Macro-economic Activity*, Harper Row, New York, 1969, pp. 185–8.

[37] Yet although most writers mention credit few are able to formulate credit variables specifically. The first attempt was Break's. See G. E. Break, *The Economic Impact of Federal Loan Insurance*, National Planning Association, Washington DC 1961. J. M. Guttentag, 'The Short Cycle in Residential Construction', *American Economic Review*, vol. 51, no. 3, 1961 also sets out a theory stressing the extreme importance of credit on the supply as well as on the demand side.

[38] L. Needleman, *The Economics of Housing,* Staples Press, London 1965, p. 128, estimates that perhaps 15 per cent of house purchases are made without borrowing from external sources. The proportion bought with the help of building societies has remained fairly constant at about two-thirds of the total annual turnover — see *UK Committee on the Working of the Monetary System* (the *Radcliffe Report*) *Memoranda of Evidence*, HMSO, London, 1960, vol. 2, part IV.

[39] In the USA house prices have risen very little, if at all, faster than the general price level and most writers in the field have therefore not taken account of this variable. In the UK, where house prices generally rise faster than general prices we expect it to be an important variable requiring separate specification rather than entering simply through deflating housing prices by the general price level.

[40] See G. F. Break, op. cit. R. F. Muth in A. C. Harberger (ed.), op. cit. also brings the effect of government behaviour indirectly via credit variables.

[41] For a brief survey of the history of US policy see e.g. J. Gillies, 'The Future of Federal Housing Policies in the United States' in A. A. Nevitt (ed.), *The Economic Problems of Housing*, Macmillan, London, 1967.

[42] Less than 2 per cent of the existing stock in the USA is owned by public authorities. The most successful programmes have been in financing house ownership, via FHA insured and VA guaranteed house programmes, rather than through direct building.

[43] See e.g. M. Nerlove, 'Distributed Lags and Estimates of Long-Run Supply and Demand Elasticities', *Journal of Farm Economics*, vol. 40, no. 2, 1958; L. R. Klein, 'The Estimation of Distributed Lags', *Econometrica*, vol. 26, no. 4, 1958 and A. Griliches, 'Distributed Lags — A Survey', *Econometrica*, vol. 35, no. 1, 1967.

[44] See Maisel's chapter on 'Non-business construction', J. S. Duesenberry et. al. (eds), *The Brookings Quarterly Econometric Model of the United States*, Rand McNally & Co., Chicago, 1965, especially pp. 183 and 191.

[45] L. M. Koyck, *Distributed Lags and Investment Analysis*, North Holland Publishing Co., Amsterdam, 1954; D. W. Jorgenson, 'Capital Theory and Investment Behaviour', *American Economic Review*, vol. LIII, no. 2, 1963 and 'Rational Distributed Lag Functions', *Econometrica*, vol. 34, no. 1, 1966.

[46] Over 20 per cent of the population in the USA moves every year. Compare this with the UK where less than 7 per cent moved per annum. See UK Social Survey No. 333, *Labour Mobility in Great Britain 1953–63*, Report by Amelia I. Harris assisted by Rosemary Claussen, HMSO, London, 1967.

[47] Although at first glance it must appear that rent control will result in disequilibrium in the market it may not. Over time suppliers may let their housing run down to such an extent that suppliers are once more on their supply schedule and the controlled price becomes the equilibrium price for the service provided. In this case price control is directly ineffective but will have affected the number and quality of houses in both the rent controlled sector and other sectors.

6 The Demand for New Housing

6.1 Introduction

We hope now to set up a model of the new private housing market which can be used to explain the structure of that market and to assess the effects on the model of changes in particular government policies. If the administrative environment remains constant and it is possible to assume no major structural changes in the housing market the model can also be used for short-term forecasting purrposes, although this of course requires that reasonable predictions can be made for all the independent variables.

The model is estimated for the period 1955 − 70 and analyses the new private housing market in Great Britain. Great Britain covers England, Wales and Scotland but not Northern Ireland. We exclude Northern Ireland because much of the data necessary is not available in the same form there as it is for Great Britain. The nature of the market is also very different and it is only a very small part of the total UK market (normally less than 3 per cent of new starts).

The starting point, 1955, was chosen partly because of data availability but also because by then most wartime controls had been removed. Immediately after the war expansion in house building was controlled by government licences which could only be obtained for private sector building with great difficulty. Controls disappeared rapidly after 1950 as did the main raw materials' shortage. By 1955 the effects of direct control had generally disappeared from the private housing market but it continued to be strongly affected by government attitudes to local authority building, general controls on interest rates and credit availability and the use of the housing sector as an aid to stabilisation policy.

The new housing market may be divided into two parts: building for private owner-occupation and building for local authorities (which is almost exclusively for rent). New building for private rental is ignored as it is a minute part of the market. In 1972 the private sector made up 61 per cent of total completions but this has varied greatly during the period of estimation, being as low as 35 per cent in 1955 when some post-war restrictions were still in force while climbing above 50 per cent in 1958 and varying between 50 per cent and 60 per cent since that date.

The demand for owner-occupied housing is, in part, for continuing housing services, as in the case of the demand for rented accommodation. However it also has another element . The ownership of a house is a store of wealth and a possible hedge against inflation neither of which aspects can be provided by rental accommodation. In a free market there would be an equilibrium clearing price relating the two markets but the administrative and financial constraints restrict this equalisation process enormously. Households obtain local authority housing on grounds of 'need' rather than by market process. On the other hand many people are excluded from owner-occupation because of imperfections in the capital market which make it impossible for all who wish to do so and are prepared to afford the payments to obtain mortgages and other finance facilities. On the demand side there is a clear distinction between the two markets because of these imperfections and it is possible therefore to build a model which concentrates on the private sector and includes the local authority sector only via the effect of total stock instead of through relative prices.

In the next chapters we present possible individual equations for demand and supply of new private housing. There are three equations necessary to describe the market:

1 The demand for completions equation.
2 The supply of starts equation.
3 The equation determining the lag structure relating the supply of starts to the supply of completions.

The demand and supply equations reflect the decision variables of purchasers and house builders while the completions/starts equation determines the time taken for dwellings to become saleable units once they are started.

6.2 Demand for completions: statistical analysis

First we consider the determinants of demand in the private new housing sector. We intend to examine only additions to the stock via new building thus simplifying the data problem.[1]

The demand for housing exhibits all the usual problems relating to durable goods. There is a demand for stock which is the demand for the ownership of existing houses and a flow demand which reflects the demand for new houses. One would expect the stock demand equation to show differences between desired and actual stock because of the difficulties and costs of adjusting demand. Buying or renting a house is a major decision taken at infrequent intervals and therefore one would expect there to be rather slow adjustment between a change in a variable determining desired demand and a change in the actual stock. The demand equation can be set out in the form:

$$ST_t - ST_{t-1} = \delta(ST_t^* - ST_{t-1}) \qquad\qquad 0 \leqslant \delta \leqslant 1$$

where $\quad ST$ = actual stock and
$\qquad ST^*$ = desired stock.[2]

The coefficient (δ) is expected to be very small, reflecting the slow adjustment of actual to desired stock demanded.

$ST_t - ST_{t-1}$ (i.e. the addition to total stock) should be made up of completions during period (t) plus those conversions which increase the number of separate dwellings less demolitions. Although there is considerable quantitative information concerning demolitions in the last few years quarterly estimates for the whole period do not exist and there is negligible information about conversions. Because of this insufficiency of data the approximation $ST_t - ST_{t-1} = C_t$, where C_t = current completions, is used throughout. The equation estimated therefore becomes:

$$C_t = f\,(ST_t^* - ST_{t-1}).$$

Desired stock is a function of economic variables such as income, the number of households, prices, etc. The demand equation will therefore have the general form:

$$C_t = f(Y, P, N, \dots, ST_{t-1}).$$

Another possibility is to estimate a flow adjustment model rather than a stock adjustment model as suggested above. The main difficulty is that the flow demand is very strongly influenced by existing stock and it is not really possible to measure the service yield from this existing stock because of variations in quality, the age structure and other attributes. If such a model were used the flow adjustment would be:

$$C_t - C_{t-1} = \gamma(C_t^* - C_{t-1}) \qquad\qquad 0 \leqslant \gamma \leqslant 1$$

so $\qquad C_t = \gamma C_t^* + (1 - \gamma)\,C_{t-1}.$

where $\quad C^* = g(Y, P, \text{etc.})$ and $C_t = ST_t - ST_{t-1}.$

The coefficient of adjustment (γ) will be very much higher than in the stock adjustment equation because the flow of new housing is only a very small proportion of total stock and can be altered over a relatively short period.

In either model we use numbers of houses as the dependent variable rather than attempt to obtain a value figure which would take into account changes in quality, age structure, etc. The assumption made is that the average value of both completions and existing stock does not change over the period. A bias is involved in that a growing proportion of the stock is post-war. Quality has increased by an estimated 4 per cent per annum in new houses over the period of the study and the average size of houses and the proportion of flats to houses has also been changing. However, because of the difficulties of measuring and taking account of these differences and because data on starts and completions are only available in terms of numbers, quantity estimates are the only possible variables to use at this stage.

The main economic variables that we hypothesise might determine the demand for new housing are net household formation, the level of incomes, the availability of substitutes and the price of housing relative to the price of other goods. Because of the way in which most house purchases are financed the actual price that the consumer pays normally includes the cost of credit so this must also be included as a determinant. Further, because of the nature of housing as an investment good, purchasers should take account of the future rate of return on the good. We therefore predict that expectations of future house prices will be an important determinant of demand.

Household formation is clearly an important underlying variable in the housing market and if it varies the demand for housing will vary directly. However there are no available statistics on household formation as such except for census years.[3] A further difficulty arises in that the rate of household formation may well be affected by the supply and price of available dwellings and thus in a full explanatory model should be regarded as partially endogenous. We did not attempt to build in such an interaction although the results would be of interest, especially for policy purposes in stress areas, because there is no time-series data.[4] A number of other available variables were tested as proxies for household formation.

The first approximation to the number of new households per quarter tried was marriages. The data is available from the Registrar General and suffers from strong seasonal variations. There are a number of reasons why it is not a good estimate of the number of households actually entering the housing market. People may enter the housing market before they get married and in this case marriage could decrease the number of houses demanded *ceteris paribus*. On the other hand many people do not set up house immediately on marriage. In this case there could be a considerable lag before they entered the housing market. These opposing effects mean that the sign on the coefficient is ambiguous. If marriages are included on the same reasoning so should deaths be. However the death of one person does not necessarily mean the dissolution of a household and there may also be lags in response to bereavement. Such variables exclude analysis of the single new household completely.

A more exact measure of the effect on housing demand could be given in terms of 'headship rates'. These have been used to provide estimates of future housing demand both in the UK and the USA.[5] However as these remain fairly constant over long periods of time, and the data would be extremely inaccurate if interpolated quarterly, there is little to be gained by using them rather than a more general measure such as the population at the time of this analysis. After a number of experiments the demand equation was estimated on the basis of completions per head of population (based on the Registrar General's annual statistics interpolated quarterly). This abstracts from the possibility of structural changes in household formation over the period.

Demand for new housing, at least in the longer run, will also be determined by the income of purchasers. As housing is a durable good there is a strong case for arguing that the determining variable is permanent rather than measured current income. When someone buys a house he continues to pay for it and derive utility from it for many years. He is therefore unlikely to take into account transitory variations in his income on which by definition he cannot rely because he has to pay regularly over a long period. Most US studies, notably Reid and Muth[6] have used Friedman's concept and calculated permanent income weights in their analyses of the American housing market. There are no such estimates of permanent income available for Great Britain.[7] The income series actually used is that of personal disposable income, as published quarterly by the Central Statistical Office. Personal disposable income was used, rather than personal income, as the amount spent on housing is normally calculated by the householder and often by the building society as a proportion of money available to spend after taxes, rather than out of total income. To take some account of the concept of permanent income a four-quarter moving average of measured income was normally employed. This was often deflated by the retail price index to obtain real income and thus purchasing power. The income variable is important not just because as income rises demand for housing, like that for all other superior goods, increases but because of the importance of building societies' controls. Building societies lend on the basis of purchasers' incomes as well as on the price and standard of the dwelling to be mortgaged. As incomes rise *ceteris paribus* the income constraint (normally that the mortgage be no more than three times the purchaser's income, plus certain other constraints) becomes less binding, and as a result the financial limitations on demand becoming effective are reduced. We therefore expect increases in income to have a twofold positive effect on demand for new housing.

As house prices rise relative to the price of other goods we hypothesise that demand for housing will decrease. The analysis however is not quite as straightforward as this for two reasons:

1 The price to the buyer is not simply the asking price but includes the cost of financing the purchase. These two aspects of demand price may not always vary together although we would expect them to affect one another.

2 As the price of housing increases there may be an effect on householders' expectations about future price increases which will affect demand both because housing is to some extent an investment good and because there may be an incentive to vary the timing of consumption. Thus inflation in general, and expected increases in house prices in particular, may have considerable influence on the demand for housing.

The importance of the level of house prices and changes in that level is such that it should be examined in more detail, and requires that we look closely at the nature of the good housing especially in a period of inflation. Housing is both a necessary good in the sense that it provides required shelter, and a luxury good in that the individual can elect to have extra services such as more space, central heating, a garden, or a garage, and may choose in many other ways to vary his consumption of housing in relation to his income and his consumption of other goods. Because of the nature of housing, reactions to price change may be difficult to analyse, even in respect to consumption.

Perhaps more importantly, an owner-occupied house as well as providing the service of accommodation is also an investment good which the purchaser buys because he believes that the rate of return is higher for this type of asset than for other available investment goods. We would, therefore, expect that demand for houses will react in different ways to changes in price depending on what mix of consumption and investment good the purchaser wishes to buy, and the relative price of housing to other consumption goods and to other investment possibilities.

If house prices rise faster than other prices we would expect a shift in demand from housing to other goods to the extent that the demand for housing is price elastic. If we look first at new owner-occupied houses, we predict that the attempted movement will be first to the closest substitute, existing owner-occupied housing. However as new and existing owner-occupied housing are very close substitutes for one another, and the owners of existing housing must live somewhere, the main effect is to increase prices in the substitute market in line with the increase in new housing. There is not likely to be much movement as a result. Some may attempt to move to housing of other tenures but such shifts are restricted by financial and institutional imperfections of the market.[8] We therefore hypothesise that most of the change in demand as a result of a relative price change will be into other goods and services such as transport and vacations.

A decrease in demand for housing as a capital asset will occur when, as a result of a price increase in the good *ceteris paribus,* the relative rate of return falls, making substitution into other available investments worthwhile. The effect may however be quite small particularly because credit available for house purchase often cannot be used to finance the purchase of other investment goods. For many people investment will be a choice between housing or nothing. Substitution effects resulting from a change of price are thus not likely to be large. Our overall hypothesis is that demand will decline as a result of house price increases, both for housing as a consumption good and as an investment good, but the size of the reaction is expected to be quite small. The effect can be included by introducing a variable which reflects the relative price of housing and other goods while measuring the real cost of housing taking account of mortgage costs.

There are no official time series data on prices of houses for sale which cover the whole period of estimation. The main sources of such information are the building societies particularly the Nationwide Building Society. Their figures relate to houses bought through the building society in each quarter so that the size of the sample varies considerably and with the economic cycle. However, it is thought that the Nationwide has perhaps the least biased sample of transactions in comparison to the other building societies.[9] The series used is that of new dwellings mortgaged by the society for which they publish an index based on 1958 as 100.

Mortgage costs can be included by multiplying the selling price by the formula by which the building societies calculate their annual repayments. This is determined by $pi^t \left[\dfrac{1-i}{1-t} \right]$ where i = the mortgage rate of interest and t = the repayment period. This can be made into a quarterly variable by calculating the rate per quarter and making 't' equal to the number of quarters in the repayment period. In using this formula we assume that

81

the mortgagor expects the rate of interest to remain constant throughout the repayment period and so takes into account the going rate. This appears to be a reasonable assumption on information grounds, especially as he expects to be compensated for variations which are the result of changes in the inflation rate. He may also expect interest rates to vary only in the long run. If so he probably has little financing difficulties resulting from such variations because building societies usually allow any changes in the rate of interest to affect the length of repayment time rather than the size of the monthly repayment. A series (*PM*) was calculated which is an index number based on the market price and the recommended building society rate of interest on new mortgages assuming a repayment period of twenty years, the normal initial repayment period.[10]

This formulation turns the price variable into a flow price (i.e. the amount the purchaser must repay each period) rather than a stock price. As most of the other independent variables are in the flow form this makes the price variable more meaningful in economic terms. The price variable was usually deflated by the retail price index to reflect changes in price relative to the prices of all other goods. A separate measure of investment good prices was not included.

The price variable, determined in the manner discussed above, reflects the normal substitution effect. If, however, relative price changes persist, we might hypothesise a further effect on the demand for housing because changes in the rate of increase of house prices cause changes in expectations about future house prices. If house prices begin to rise more rapidly and are expected to continue to do so the incentive to buy now rather than in the future is increased. Further, if house prices rise more rapidly than other investment good prices and the future is expected to be like the present, the incentive to invest in housing as an asset is also increased. Looking at housing as a consumption good a purchaser must weigh the cost of moving housing expenditure forward, given the change in price, against spending an equivalent amount on another form of investment and realising this investment to pay the increased price of housing in the future. He could also decide to leave decisions about future consumption until the future. His decision will depend upon his expectation of relative price rises. If purchasers expect house prices to increase in the future then they will substitute current for future housing expenditure. If they expect them to increase faster than other goods they will substitute housing investment for other forms of investment. If, on the other hand, the increases are expected to stop, people will regard housing as a currently expensive good for which other goods should be substituted.[11] Hedging against future price increases will normally increase the demand for housing now, but a price increase now could have either a positive or a negative effect on purchasers' expectations of future prices and therefore their desire to hedge. The size of this effect is also uncertain depending on the nature of the expectations, especially those relating to relative prices, and the ability to put desires into reality through access to finance in the housing market rather than to other sectors of the economy. It should be remembered also that if a change in the rate of inflation causes a structural change in the timing of expenditure for hedging purposes the rates of return on all investments will be varied leading to further decision changes about the relative benefits of consumption and investment.

We include this effect by including the rate of change of prices. In some formulations the rate of change in general prices $\left[\dfrac{R_t - R_{t-1}}{R_{t-1}} \right]$ is used to discover whether overall inflation causes a shift into housing demand. In others the rate of change of house prices itself is used to reflect the expected return on the good actually being purchased. By including either of these variables we assume that most people believe the future will be like the present, for we are using the actual rate as an indicator of the expected rate of change of prices.

Many authors[12] have argued that financial costs enter as availability constraints as well as price changes because building societies are loath to vary the mortgage rates of interest very often and therefore operate a number of non-price controls which affect effective demand. Building societies operate two main non-price constraints on lending. They vary the amount that they will lend to a particular purchaser on the basis of his income, family circumstances, and type of house he wishes to buy, and they vary the total they will lend in any one period in response to the financial resources they have available. The constraint on how much an individual purchaser may borrow is determined by the relationship between his money income and the price of the house he wishes to buy. If house prices rise faster than money incomes the constraint becomes more binding and over the last ten years this has perhaps been the general case.[13] There also seems little doubt that building societies vary the severity by which they apply their rules depending on the general ease of credit.[14] The strength of the constraint is therefore related not only to the relative increase of house prices in comparison to incomes, but also to the extent of monetary controls in the economy. When the government introduces a credit squeeze, building societies find it difficult to obtain finance at their share rate of interest. However they do not wish to increase this interest rate because of the costs involved in changing the rate, and they thus have less money available to offer mortgagors and rationing is enforced. When credit becomes easier liquidity flows in and they are glad to lend on far less stringent terms without necessarily changing the price.

Their methods of rationing in times of stringency are not clearly defined. They include tightening the application of price/income ratios, reducing the proportion of the valuation of the property they are prepared to advance, and increasing the severity of restrictions on the type and quality of housing on which they will lend. All those tend to reduce effective demand. If, ultimately, the building societies do increase the mortgage rate, any small change in the rate of interest will have a significant effect on the size of the monthly repayment because loans are for twenty to twenty-five years.[15] Thus government monetary controls reduce the availability of building society credit and tighten the constraint of their lending rules. Both these effects increase the real cost of house purchase and so reduce effective demand.

We hypothesise that variations in the extent to which non-price constraints are imposed by the building societies vary with the availability of credit to the building societies. There are a number of possible measures of this availability. The most obvious variable to include to reflect this constraint is the net flow of funds into building societies. The rationale is that building societies are required to keep a given reserve ratio and therefore in the longer run can only lend out what they get in. Alterations in the flow of funds will thus force changes in building societies' lending policy decisions. It is possible however that such a measure will not adequately reflect the timing of policy changes because building societies are rarely at the margin of their lending ability and are able to vary their reserve ratio in response to changes in the flow of funds at least in the short run.

Because O'Herlihy and Spencer[16] felt the flow of funds an inadequate explanatory variable they devised a different measure of the building societies' credit constraint. They constructed two dummies reflecting 'mild' and 'strict' rationing on the basis of qualitative comment about mortgage availability in leading economic and financial journals. The main drawback of such dummies is that they are obtained by using ex-post information and say nothing about the actual determinants of building societies' behaviour. They therefore act as non-explanatory surrogates for building societies' rational or irrational decision making. The flow of funds on the other hand is a 'real' determining factor, not a dummy substitute for other, unknown variables. It is only as a result of actually estimating the demand equation that we will be able to assess (a) whether non-price credit availability constraints are important in determining housing demand and (b) whether the better explanatory power is obtained by using the flow of funds or these rationing dummies.

The last economic variable which we hypothesise may be important in determining the demand for new housing is the existing stock of dwellings. This reflects the availability of the closest substitute for new housing: that of dwellings already built. It is through this stock variable that the effect of changes in local authority or private rental provision is expected to be felt reflecting a quantity rather than a price effect because these markets are so strongly controlled. The Department of the Environment has now produced annual time-series data for the number of existing dwellings available in Great Britain at quarterly intervals. This is used, usually deflated by population as is the dependent variable completions. The demand equation is thus normally estimated as demand per head of population.

Finally dummies were included to remove seasonality.[17] (This is fairly strong in the dependent variable and also in some of the independent variables.) Another dummy was included for the first quarter of 1963 in which construction work came almost completely to a halt because of the excessive cold.

6.3 Statistical estimation

The estimation procedure used in determining the model was first to test each equation as a separate unit by single-stage least-squares methods and then, having defined a possible structure for each equation, to examine the interactive nature of the model using two-staged least-squares methods to remove bias. In this chapter we report on the ordinary least-squares results for the demand equation. The actual coefficients will, of course, be biased but the general structure should be clear.

A number of formulations of the demand equation were estimated to try and define some of the hypotheses which could not be specified on the basis of theoretical analysis alone and to test the significance of those which could. We looked first at the form of the income variable. The choice here lies between real and money income per head. In theory we usually assume that people determine their consumption of a good on the basis of their real income. So the variable to be included should be personal disposable income per head deflated by the general retail price index. In the case of housing there is an extra complication in that building societies determine how much they will lend a client partly on the basis of the relationship between his income and the price of the dwelling. If we hypothesise that this constraint affects purchasers' decisions there is a case

Table 6.1

Stock adjustment demand equation
Dependent variable PC/N_t

(61 observations, seasonal dummies and dummy for first quarter 1963 included in all estimates)

1   $6\cdot12$ $(1\cdot93)$ $+$ $13\cdot61\,Y/N_t$ $(2\cdot35)$ $-$ $4\cdot48\,PM/R_t$ $(-0\cdot34)$ $-$ $2\cdot87\,DW_t$ $(-1\cdot29)$ $-$ $20\cdot08\,ST/N_{t-1}$ $(-1\cdot76)$

$\bar{r}^2 = 0\cdot46 \quad DW = 0\cdot20$

2   $8\cdot45$ $(2\cdot71)$ $+$ $20\cdot93\,Y/N_{t-2}$ $(3\cdot24)$ $-$ $16\cdot68\,PM/R_t$ $(-1\cdot20)$ $-$ $2\cdot48\,DW$ $(-1\cdot17)$ $-$ $28\cdot40\,ST/N_{t-1}$ $(-2\cdot53)$

$\bar{r}^2 = 0\cdot50 \quad DW = 0\cdot25$

3   $7\cdot35$ $(2\cdot66)$ $+$ $26\cdot03\,Y/N_{t-2}$ $(4\cdot97)$ $-$ $47\cdot00\,PM/R_{t-2}$ $(-3\cdot90)$ $-$ $1\cdot55\,DW_t$ $(-0\cdot82)$ $-$ $24\cdot06\,ST/N_{t-1}$ $(-2\cdot41)$

$\bar{r}^2 = 0\cdot61 \quad DW = 0\cdot38$

4   $3\cdot10$ $(3\cdot53)$ $+$ $3310\cdot68\,YRP_t$ $(13\cdot17)$ $-$ $3\cdot49\,PM/R_t$ $(-0\cdot59)$ $+$ $0\cdot57\,DW_t$ $(0\cdot51)$ $-$ $15\cdot74\,ST/N_{t-1}$ $(-4\cdot64)$

$\bar{r}^2 = 0\cdot86 \quad DW = 0\cdot68$

5   $1\cdot78$ $(1\cdot98)$ $+$ $3356\cdot01\,YRP_{t-2}$ $(12\cdot39)$ $-$ $13\cdot52\,PM/R_t$ $(-3\cdot10)$ $-$ $1\cdot46\,DW_t$ $(-1\cdot25)$ $-$ $10\cdot66\,ST/N_{t-1}$ $(-3\cdot12)$

$\bar{r}^2 = \quad DW = 0\cdot75$

6   $0\cdot47$ $+$ $3219\cdot23\,YRP_{t-2}$ $(13\cdot31)$ $-$ $21\cdot66\,PM/R_{t-2}$ $(-3\cdot53)$ $-$ $1\cdot11\,DW_t$ $(-1\cdot03)$ $-$ $5\cdot55\,ST/N_{t-1}$ $(-1\cdot53)$

$\bar{r}^2 = 0\cdot87 \quad DW = 0\cdot93$

for using money income, which affects the building societies' decisions, instead of the more usual real income variable in the demand equation.

We also concentrated on examining possible lag structures which might reflect the rapidity by which purchasers react to changes in the independent variables. We have no prior hypothesis about the likely length of such lags on the independent variables. It may be that consumers change their demand on the basis of their current income, which is the one that the building societies take into account. Even here there could be a short lag as purchasers may obtain their mortgage well before actual sale. Moreover perception about income, and changes in income, may mean that there is a lagged response. Costs of moving will also be important in affecting the timing of house purchase decisions and one would expect these to cause a threshold effect and therefore a lagged response. The same factors could well influence purchasers' reactions to changes in house prices, especially as here there is also need to gather information, a time-consuming and costly process. Even the consumer's method of formulating his response to inflation may be based on out-of-date information which would result in a lagged relationship between demand and the rate of change of price variable.

Table 6.1 shows the first results of estimating the stock adjustment demand equation. Using current economic variables including money income we find the expected sign on income (Y/N_t) and price (PM/R_t) and a negative sign on the inflation variable (DW) suggesting a possible precautionary response to the rate of change of general prices (equation 1). If the income variable is lagged two periods significance increases (equation 2) as it does if price is also lagged two quarters (equation 3). The third equation gives the most promising results: a positive and significant response to income, a negative and significant response to price and a significant coefficient on stock (ST/N_{t-1}). The coefficient on the inflation variable is not significant in any of the formulations suggesting that purchasers do not react greatly to changes in general prices except in relation to the relative price of houses.

When real rather than money income is included the significance of the variable increases very considerably (equation 4) but it is not further increased by introducing lagged rather than current income. However, the effect of price is far more significant when a six-month lag is introduced (equation 6, suggesting that there are problems of information flow when determining demand. The rate of change of prices is still insignificant in all formulations, but the sign is not always negative.

Table 6.2 sets out the comparable equations for the flow adjustment demand structure. Again real income gives better results than money in-

87

Table 6.2

Flow adjustment demand equation
Dependent variable PC/N_t

(59 observations, seasonal dummies and dummy for first quarter 1963 included in all estimates)

1
$$2\cdot29 + 6\cdot18\, Y/N_t - 11\cdot44\, PM/R_t - 1\cdot96\, DW_t - 7\cdot66\, ST/N_{t-1}$$
$$(1\cdot90)\quad (2\cdot81)\quad\quad (-2\cdot31)\quad\quad (-2\cdot36)\quad\quad (-1\cdot77)$$
$$+0\cdot91\, PC/N_{t-1}$$
$$(17\cdot96)$$

$\bar{r}^2 = 0\cdot92$ $DW = 1\cdot89$

2
$$1\cdot68 + 7\cdot30\, Y/N_{t-2} - 18\cdot81\, PM/R_{t-2} - 1\cdot57\, DW_t - 5\cdot27\, ST/N_{t-1}$$
$$(1\cdot37)\quad (2\cdot90)\quad\quad (-3\cdot48)\quad\quad (-1\cdot98)\quad\quad (-1\cdot20)$$
$$+0\cdot84\, PC/N_{t-1}$$
$$(15\cdot55)$$

$\bar{r}^2 = 0\cdot93$ $DW = 1\cdot90$

3
$$0\cdot98 + 1452\cdot03\, YRP_t - 6\cdot08\, PM/R_t - 0\cdot59\, DW_t - 3\cdot81\, ST/N_{t-1}$$
$$(1\cdot65)\quad (5\cdot65)\quad\quad (-1\cdot64)\quad\quad (-0\cdot83)\quad\quad (-2\cdot26)$$
$$+0\cdot63\, PC/N_{t-1}$$
$$(9.12)$$

$\bar{r}^2 = 0\cdot95$ $DW = 1\cdot72$

4
$$0\cdot58 + 1382\cdot66\, YRP_t - 8\cdot15\, PM/R_{t-2} - 0\cdot57\, DW_t - -3\cdot81\, ST/N_{t-1}$$
$$(0\cdot89)\quad (5\cdot45)\quad\quad (-2\cdot11)\quad\quad (-0\cdot81)\quad\quad - (-1\cdot43)$$
$$+\ 0\cdot62\, PC/N_{t-1}$$
$$(9\cdot20)$$

$\bar{r}^2 = 0\cdot95$ $DW = 1\cdot75$

5
$$0\cdot72 + 1361\cdot10\, YRP_t - 7\cdot31\, PM/R_t + 0\cdot67\, DP_t - 4\cdot29\, ST/N_{t-1}$$
$$(1\cdot22)\quad (5\cdot35)\quad\quad (-2\cdot10)\quad\quad (1\cdot86)\quad\quad (-1\cdot78)$$
$$+\ 0\cdot63\, PC_{t-1}/N$$
$$(9\cdot48)$$

$\bar{r}^2 = 0\cdot95$ $DW = 1\cdot56$

6
$$-0\cdot32 + 1068\cdot66\, YRP_t - 11\cdot99\, PM/R_t + 0\cdot83\, DP + 0\cdot69\, PC/N_{t-1}$$
$$(-3\cdot59)\quad (5\cdot38)\quad\quad (-5\cdot16)\quad\quad (2\cdot32)\quad\quad (11\cdot60)$$

$\bar{r}^2 = 0\cdot95$ $DW = 1\cdot60$

7
$$-0\cdot34 + 1220\cdot98\, YRP_{t-2} - 13\cdot76\, PM/R_{t-2} + 0\cdot79\, DP_t + 0\cdot62\, PC/N_{t-1}$$
$$(-3\cdot30)\quad (4\cdot86)\quad\quad (-4\cdot84)\quad\quad (2\cdot11)\quad\quad (8\cdot55)$$

$\bar{r}^2 = 0\cdot94$ $DW = 1\cdot46$

---

come but in this formulation current income is normally more significant than lagged income. This may reflect the more perfect nature of the new housing market especially in relation to information flow in comparison to the market dealing in the whole housing stock. The coefficient on the price variable still suggests that there may be a lag in purchasers' reactions to changes in price.

Within the flow model the coefficient on stock is sometimes insignificant, suggesting that there is little interaction between the market for existing stock and that for new housing. This would have quite important policy implications, for instance in examining the relationship between changes in public sector building (which enters through the stock variable) and private housing demand. These implications require further analysis and testing.

The last modification made at this stage was to substitute the rate of change of house prices for the general inflation variable. The coefficient on this variable (DP) was found to be positive and significant suggesting that purchasers see housing as a good investment when its price rises basing their expectations about future returns on investment on the current rate of price change of the good they are purchasing. This difference in sign between DW and DP is of considerable interest for it suggests that consumers are perhaps precautionary in their reactions to general inflation but speculative in relation to changes in house prices, i.e. in respect of the good they are actually buying.

The most difficult and intractable problem which arises from examination of these estimates is that of auto-correlation. The Durbin-Watson statistic is very low indeed in the stock-adjustment equation, suggesting the existence of strong positive auto-correlation. The Durbin-Watson statistic is far closer to two in the flow adjustment equation but as the structure inherently includes the lagged dependent variable this cannot automatically be interpreted as implying that there is little autocorrelation. [18] It was therefore decided to test for auto-correlation of both first and greater orders and to re-compute the demand equation once such auto-correlation has been removed. [19]

Another problem may be that of multi-collinearity between the independent variables, partially as a result of the method of measurement chosen for real income, relative prices and the rate of change of prices all of which include the general price level, and partially because of the real relationship which exists between prices (especially house prices) and income. The instability of the estimated variables suggests that multi-collinearity may be a problem but it could simply be the result of clear auto-correlation bias.

To remove the problem of autocorrelation, and to estimate its significance, various versions of the demand equation were re-estimated using RALS and testing for all possible combinations of autocorrelation up to seventh order. In no case was autocorrelation above first-order significant. The coefficients of auto-correlation on the stock adjustment equations were found to be extremely significant and very close to one, with 't' statistics usually over fifteen. Once the autocorrelation was removed the re-estimated equations had very different coefficients from the original estimates. On the other hand when the flow adjustment structure was tested normally not even first-order autocorrelation was significant. So when what autocorrelation there was was removed there was little change in the value of the independent coefficients. However in order to estimate the full model when there is autocorrelation elsewhere, and for general comparability, it is necessary for the flow demand equation to be estimated removing first-order autocorrelation. Of course, even though the autocorrelation is not significant, its removal will make the estimates more efficient.

Table 6.3

Demand for completions – stock equations, first – order autocorrelation removed

Dependent variable = PC/N_t

(59 observations, seasonal dummies and dummy for first quarter of 1963 included in all estimates)

1	4·39 + (1·97)	1441·94 YRP_t + (3·05)	9·35 PMR_t (1·17)	+ 0·48 DW_t (0·76)	− 15·50 ST/N_{t-1} (2·15)
		alpha 1 = 0·91 (13·73)	$s = 0·038$		
2	3·49 + (0·79	801·01 YRP_{t-2}− (1·72)	3·40 PMR_{t-2} (0·41)	− 0·39 DW_t (0·66)	− 9·50 ST/N_{t-1} (0·75)
		alpha 1 = 0·95 (17·14)	$s = 0·041$		
3	3·24 + (1·00)	1231 YRP_t (2·94)	− 2·97 PMR_{t-2} (0·37)	+ 0·43 DP_t (1·69)	− 10·18 ST/N_{t-1} (1·03)
		alpha 1 = 0·93 (15·14)	$s = 0·038$		
4	3·18 + (0·69)	830·04 YRP_{t-2}− (1·86)	7·89 PMR_{t-2} (0·94)	+ 0·52 DP_t (1·95)	− 8·24 ST/N_{t-1} (0·62)
		alpha 1 = 0·95 (17·18)	$s = 0·039$		

Tables 6.3 and 6.4 show some of the comparable results to Tables 6.1 and 6.2 when first-order autocorrelation is removed using GIVE.[20] Now in the stock adjustment equations current price including mortgage costs is always positive reflecting more a general trend variable than the true effect of price. When a lag of two periods is introduced the effect of an increase in price is negative as hypothesised. It is not however normally significant perhaps reflecting our earlier suggestions that substitution effects might be quite small. There appears to be some multicollinearity between income and price for as longer lags on real income are introduced the significance of price lagged two periods increases. This is not really surprising as both are deflated by the general price level. It also becomes clearer when autocorrelation is removed that the effect of inflation is far better reflected by the rate of change of house prices than by that of general prices, the coefficient on which is not significantly different from zero. The best estimate appears to be Table 6.3, equation 4. The great weakness is in the price variable which needs further examination especially in relation to the cost of credit. This suggests that too many conflicting reactions are being bound together in a single variable.

The estimates for the flow adjustment demand equation are given in Table 6.4. When we look at the new housing market entirely on its own lagged prices have a more significant effect than current prices. Even with current prices however the sign is negative as hypothesised although insignificant. Prices and incomes show slight multicollinearity as expected because of their structure. The effect of the rate of change of general prices is negative and insignificant implying if anything precautionary behaviour but when the rate of change of new house prices is included the effect is positive as hypothesised and nearly always significant at the 5 per cent level. Existing stock has a considerably less significant coefficient than before first-order autoregression was removed implying that to a great extent it had reflected a trend variable and that existing stock does not have great importance in determining demand in the new housing market in the short run.

The results suggest that further analysis of the effects of house prices relative to general prices, the mortgage rate and availability of credit would help to improve the specification of the demand equation and so next we included measures of availability and rationing in the demand equation estimates.

The two measures of credit rationing that we suggested in the analysis section were the net inflow of funds into building societies and the dummy variables constructed by Spencer and O'Herlihy. The flow of funds is a real economic variable but not necessarily the only one of importance to have

Table 6.4

Demand for completions — flow equations, first-order autocorrelation removed

(59 observations, seasonal dummies and dummy for first quarter 1963 included in all estimates)

1 $1.62 + 1712.61\ YRP_t - 3.56\ PMR_t - 0.22\ DW_t - 8.09\ ST/N_{t-1}$
$(1.70)\quad (4.60)\qquad\quad (0.67)\qquad\quad (0.27)\qquad\quad (2.11)$
$+\ 0.53\ PC/N_{t-1}$
(4.55)

alpha 1 = 0.28 $s = 0.037$

2 $0.94 + 1564.94\ YRP_t - 7.06\ PMR_{t-2} - 0.34\ DW_t - 5.35\ ST/N_{t-1}$
$(1.00)\quad (4.42)\qquad\quad (1.42)\qquad\qquad (0.43)\qquad\quad (1.40)$
$+\ 0.56\ PC/N_{t-1}$
(5.50)

alpha 1 = 0.20 $s = 0.372$
(1.03)

3 $-0.14 + 1467.59\ YRP_{t-2} - 13.88\ PMR_{t-2} - 1.12\ DW_t - 1.04\ ST/N_{t-1}$
$(0.17)\quad (4.18)\qquad\qquad (2.65)\qquad\qquad (1.55)\qquad\quad (0.31)$
$+\ 0.56\ PC/N_{t-1}$
(5.42)

alpha 1 = 0.23 $s = 0.039$
(1.34)

4 $1.40 + 1610.89\ YRP_t - 4.40\ PMR_t + 0.75\ DP_t - 7.06\ ST/N_{t-1}$
$(1.52)\quad (4.92)\qquad\quad (0.83)\qquad\quad (2.33)\qquad\quad (1.94)$
$+\ 0.52\ PC/N_{t-1}$
(5.18)

alpha 1 = 0.34 $s = 0.035$
(1.91)

5 $1.03 + 1551.44\ YRP_t - 6.40\ PMR_{t-2} + 0.73\ DP_t - 5.58\ ST/N_{t-1}$
$(1.08)\quad (4.72)\qquad\quad (1.22)\qquad\qquad (2.31)\qquad\quad (1.46)$
$+\ 0.52\ PC/N_{t-1}$
(5.46)

alpha 1 = 0.33 $s = 0.035$
(1.80)

6 $-0.09 + 1463.42\ YRP_{t-2} - 13.93\ PMR_{t-2} + 0.87\ DP_t - 1.09\ ST/N_{t-1}$
$(0.10)\quad (4.05)\qquad\qquad (2.49)\qquad\qquad (2.68)\qquad\quad (0.30)$
$+\ 0.50\ PC/N_{t-1}$
(4.64)

alpha 1 = 0.37 $s = 0.037$
(2.14)

7 $-0.37 + 1225.91\ YRP_t - 13.01\ PMR_t + 0.91\ DP_t + 0.61\ PC/N_{t-1}$
$(3.07)\quad (4.65)\qquad\quad (4.30)\qquad\quad (2.71)\qquad\quad (6.93)$

alpha 1 = 0.29 $s = 0.036$
(1.60)

8 $-0.36 + 1242.30\ YRP_t - 13.02\ PMR_{t-2} + 0.81\ DP_t + 0.57\ PC/N_{t-1}$
$(3.21)\quad (6.32)\qquad\quad (4.70)\qquad\qquad (2.48)\qquad\quad (6.69)$

alpha 1 = 0.30 $s = 0.035$
(1.77)

effect on building society behaviour. There is a problem in determining how rapidly the change in availability of funds to building societies leads to a change in the availability of mortgages and thus demand. The dummies on the other hand are ex-post surrogates for building society behaviour, the determinants of which have not been included in the model. They are therefore of little use for forecasting future trends or for explaining the true structure of building societies' financial behaviour.

In the stock adjustment model we took equation 4 in Table 6.3 and added first the dummies for credit rationing and second different lengths of lag on the net flow of funds variable. The results are presented in Table 6.5. The inclusion of MR and SR for medium and strong rationing increases the significance of all other variables but are themselves insignificant. They do however have the hypothesised negative sign (equation 1). The 's' value is not reduced showing the explanatory power has not been increased and it remains a generally unsatisfactory equation.

Table 6.5

The effects of credit availability — stock adjustment demand equation

(59 observations, seasonal and first quarter 1963 dummies)

1     $2 \cdot 42 + 930 \cdot 09 \, YRP_{t-2} - 8 \cdot 51 \, PMR_{t-2} + 0 \cdot 55 \, DP_t - 0 \cdot 01 \, MR$
      $(0 \cdot 63) \quad (2 \cdot 00) \quad\quad (0 \cdot 99) \quad\quad (2 \cdot 01) \quad\quad (0 \cdot 71)$

                                         $- 0 \cdot 01 \, SR - 6 \cdot 20 \, ST/N_{t-1}$
                                         $(0 \cdot 72) \quad (0 \cdot 55)$

             alpha 1 = 0·94 $s = 0 \cdot 04$
                 (14·97)

2     $3 \cdot 66 + 803 \cdot 35 \, YRP_{t-2} - 7 \cdot 41 \, PMR_{t-2} + 0 \cdot 49 \, DP_t + 0 \cdot 0001 \, FF_{t-2}$
      $(0 \cdot 76) \quad (1 \cdot 78) \quad\quad (0 \cdot 88) \quad\quad (1 \cdot 84) \quad\quad (0 \cdot 64)$

                                         $- 9 \cdot 68 \, ST/N_{t-1}$
                                         $(0 \cdot 69)$

             alpha 1 = 0·95 $s = 0 \cdot 04$
                 (17·55)

3     $5 \cdot 26 + 605 \cdot 04 \, YRP_{t-2} - 2 \cdot 76 \, PMR_{t-2} + 0 \cdot 50 \, DP_t + 0 \cdot 0003 \, FF_{t-3}$
      $(1 \cdot 01) \quad (1 \cdot 34) \quad\quad (0 \cdot 32) \quad\quad (1 \cdot 94) \quad\quad (1 \cdot 72)$

                                         $- 14 \cdot 35 \, ST/N_{t-1}$
                                         $(0 \cdot 97)$

             alpha 1 = 0·95 $s = 0 \cdot 039$
                 (20·92)

When the flow of funds is included it has the hypothesised sign but is not significant at the 5 per cent level. It also has little effect on the other variables. The flow of funds lagged three periods (equation 3) gives the best results. It reduces the already insignificant coefficient on price suggesting that part of the cost of credit variable is replaced by the availability variable as might be expected. This version also leaves the value of 's' unchanged rather than worsening it as happens if shorter or longer lags on the flow of funds are included. On this evidence we suggest that building societies do change their behaviour in response to the flow of funds but that their reaction is not of overwhelming importance in determining demand, as some earlier commentators have suggested. In general the stock adjustment formulation is not very satisfactory with or without rationing variables. To examine the behaviour of the whole owner-occupied market far more attempts should be made to look at interactions between markets and other causes of changes in stock. This requires a far more complex model, outside our competence at the present time mainly because of the lack of data.

When we turn to the flow adjustment model the results are far more satisfactory. The estimates are shown in Table 6.6. Equation 1 is strictly comparable with equation 7 in Table 6.4. The inclusion of the flow of funds lagged three periods decreases the value of 's' by about 3 per cent and reduces the size of the alpha coefficient. Both suggest that this is the best specified equation. The values on the coefficients of income, the rate of change of house prices and lagged completions are only marginally affected by the inclusion of the flow of funds suggesting little multi-collinearity while the coefficient on FF_{t-3} has the correct sign and is itself significant at the 5 per cent level. Rather oddly both the value of the coefficient and the significance of the price and mortgage costs of housing increase. This suggests a better specification of price but also that availability is complementary to the cost of credit rather than a substitute. Similar effects occur when lagged rather than current price is used (equation 2, in comparison with equation 8, Table 6.4).

When existing stock is included as an independent variable (equations 3 and 4 — which have the same specification as equations 4 and 5 in Table 6.4) we again observe an increase in the value and significance of the price variable. The flow of funds is also more significant perhaps reflecting the problems of selling an existing dwelling in order to buy a new house. The value of 's' is reduced by over 5 per cent and all variables except the price are significant at the 5 per cent level. Current price is significant only at the 10 per cent level. The inclusion of the flow of funds increases the overall explanatory power of the flow adjustment demand equation. The

94

Table 6.6

The effect of credit availability — flow adjustment demand equation

(59 observations, seasonal and first quarter 1963 dummies)

---

1 -0.27 $+$ $1124.33\ YRP_t$ $-$ $15.65\ PMR_t$ $+$ $0.95\ DP_t$ $+$ $0.0003\ FF_{t-3}$
   (2.49) (5.00) (5.20) (2.64) (2.00)

   $+$ $0.65\ PC/N_{t-1}$
       (9.08)

   alpha 1 $= 0.15$ $s = 0.035$
            (0.87)

2 -0.26 $+$ $1137.85\ YRP_t$ $-$ $14.81\ PMR_{t-1}$ $+$ $0.82\ DP_t$ $+$ $0.0002\ FF_{t-3}$
   (2.41) (5.11) (5.34) (2.40) (1.72)

   $+$ $0.60\ PC/N_{t-1}$
       (8.08)

   alpha 1 $= 0.20$ $s = 0.035$
            (1.20)

3 1.75 $+$ $1590.29\ YRP_t$ $-$ $7.03\ PMR_t$ $+$ $0.79\ DP_t$ $+$ $0.0004\ FF_{t-3}$
   (2.10) (5.60) (1.51) (2.43) (2.63)

   $-$ $8.03\ ST/N_{t-1}$ $+$ $0.54\ PC/N_{t-1}$
       (2.47) (6.43)

   alpha 1 $= 0.22$ $s = 0.033$
            (1.24)

4 1.75 $+$ $1583.65\ YRP_t$ $-$ $6.36\ PMR_{t-2}$ $+$ $0.75\ DP_t$ $+$ $0.0003\ FF_{t-3}$
   (1.82) (5.32) (1.30) (2.39) (2.36)

   $-$ $7.99\ ST/N_{t-1}$ $+$ $0.51\ PC/N_{t-1}$
       (2.12) (6.07)

   alpha 1 $= 0.27$ $s = 0.033$
            (1.57)

5 -0.21 $+$ $879.14\ YRP_t$ $-$ $9.52\ PMR_t$ $+$ $1.04\ DP_t$ $-$ $0.02\ MR$ $-$ $0.03\ SR$
   (1.65) (3.27) (3.06) (2.79) (1.56) (1.89)

   $+$ $0.69\ PC/N_{t-1}$
       (9.30)

   alpha 1 $= 0.11$ $s = 0.036$
            (0.63)

6 1.15 $+$ $1312\ YRP_t$ $-$ $3.82\ PMR_t$ $+$ $0.87\ DP_t$ $-$ $0.02\ MR$ $-$ $0.02\ SR$
   (1.38) (3.70) (0.79) (2.47) (1.20) (1.22)

   $-$ $5.63\ ST/N_{t-1}$ $+$ $0.59\ PC/N_{t-1}$
       (1.69) (6.14)

   alpha 1 $= 0.22$ $s = 0.035$
            (1.20)

---

main question raised by the results is whether the original formulation of the price variable as a quarterly cost of purchase including mortgage costs hides more than it explains. Now that it is clear that the difference between the effects of cost and availability of credit are of importance it may well be necessary to separate the price variable so that the two effects can be fully analysed, even though we hypothesised that the decision is made in relation to the two taken together.

The equation was estimated using both shorter and longer lags on the net flow of funds. In no case was the significance of the variable or of the equation as a whole increased.

In equations 5 and 6 the effect of including the Spencer and O'Herlihy dummies is shown. The results are comparable with equations 7 and 4 in Table 6.4. In neither version does their inclusion increase the explanatory power of the equation and the coefficients on the dummies themselves are not significant. Rather surprisingly the strong rationing variable has very little more effect than that of medium rationing. In both cases the value of the price variable is decreased suggesting that there is, as expected, multicollinearity between the rate of interest and the dummy variables. The results suggest that the ex-post construction of the dummy variables is not fully able to take account of building societies' behaviour in relation to credit rationing but rather reflects the effect of monetary controls in general which also affects the rate of interest.

The results of testing various formulations using different rationing variables suggest that credit availability is an important, but by no means an all important, determinant of the demand for new housing. In later work when estimating the full model we will normally include the real economic variable, the net flow of funds, rather than the Spencer and O'Herlihy dummies. Evidence on lags suggests that the effect is slow working, as changes in the net flow of funds into building societies are not reflected in changes in demand for houses for about nine months, but are still significant.

6.4   Another possible demand structure

The original rationale for using house prices including mortgage costs as the price variable was that purchasers base their demand on what they wish to pay out in monthly repayments. These include both capital and interest costs. Yet this method hides the precise relationship between purchase price and monthly repayment. As there also appear to be important relationships between the cost and availability of credit and their effect on demand there may be a case for trying an alternative formulation of the demand equation introducing price and the mortgage rate of interest separately.

Another problem of the specification used so far is that it will not be possible to calculate two-staged least-squares estimates without modifications because the price variable will not be defined in the same way in the supply equation. As a result we have to linearise the demand equation and separate out the price variable before least-squares bias can be removed. It was decided to re-estimate the best formulated flow adjustment demand equation in a way which separates out each variable, i.e. $PC_t = f(Y_t, P_t, BSM_t, DP, ...)$. This removes all problems for the two staged least-squares estimation process. It however includes $\dfrac{P_t - P_{t-1}}{P_{t-1}}$ which must be treated as endogenously determined. This causes no difficulty for two-staged least-squares estimates but will have to be linearised when we wish to simulate the model.

This simpler formulation also allows us to determine the effect of the population variable separately and means that the estimation of the whole equation is now in terms of the absolute number of completions per quarter, PC, rather than in terms of completions per head of population.

The estimates of the demand for completions using this structure are shown in Tables 6.7 and 6.8. Table 6.7 assumes that we are interested mainly in short-term variables defined in money rather than in real terms. The results are not easily compared with the earlier estimates because of the changes in the relative size of coefficients. In terms of the significance of individual coefficients the most important result is that the price variable is insignificant while the mortgage rate is very significant. This suggests that in the earlier formulation the actual price was dominated by the payment of twenty years' worth of interest. It suggests that demand reactions to changes in the purchase price are very limited indeed. The estimates with the greatest explanatory value occur when both price and the mortgage rate are lagged by two periods. The lag probably reflects the nature of the decision process by which demanders often obtain their mortgage well before the actual completion date. However the relative irregularity in changes of the mortgage rate mean that little stress should be put on the result.

When the availability of credit is included (equations 3–6) the importance of the mortgage rate is hardly reduced at all. The inclusion of the rationing dummies reduces the value of 's' by about 5 per cent and the coefficients are themselves significant. However the amount by which

Table 6.7

Demand for completions 1956–70
Dependent variable PC_t

(59 observations, seasonal dummies and dummy for first quarter 1963 included in all estimates)

---

1    $22{,}216$ $+ \;\; 4{\cdot}31\, Y_t$ $+ \;\; 54268\, DP_t$ $- \;\; 1367470\, BSM_{t-2}$ $- \;\; 61{\cdot}99\, P_{t-2}$
     $(4{\cdot}50)$ $(2{\cdot}36)$ $(2{\cdot}64)$ $(3{\cdot}56)$ $(0{\cdot}89)$

                                                   $+ \;\; 0{\cdot}70\, PC_{t-1}$
                                                      $(9{\cdot}87)$

       alpha $1 = 0{\cdot}16$ $s = 2078$
            $(1{\cdot}05)$

2    $22{,}488$ $+ \;\; 5{\cdot}82\, Y_{t-2}$ $+ \;\; 56488\, DP_t$ $- \;\; 1396868\, BSM_{t-2}$ $- \;\; 102{\cdot}29\, P_{t-2}$
     $(4{\cdot}55)$ $(2{\cdot}47)$ $(2{\cdot}82)$ $(3{\cdot}63)$ $(1{\cdot}24)$

                                                    $+ \;\; 0{\cdot}68\, PC_{t-1}$
                                                      $(9{\cdot}17)$

       alpha $1 = 0{\cdot}17$ $s = 2066$
            $(1{\cdot}12)$

3    $22{,}420$ $+ \;\; 3{\cdot}69\, Y_t$ $- \;\; 69{\cdot}72\, P_{t-2}$ $- \;\; 1284694\, BSM_{t-2}$ $+ \;\; 51761\, DP$
     $(4{\cdot}89)$ $(2{\cdot}16)$ $(1{\cdot}09)$ $(3{\cdot}56)$ $(2{\cdot}33)$

                                       $+ \;\; 11{\cdot}24\, FF_{t-2}$ $+ \;\; 0{\cdot}74\, PC_{t-1}$
                                           $(1{\cdot}36)$ $(11{\cdot}04)$

       alpha $1 = 0{\cdot}04$ $s = 2068$
            $(0{\cdot}28)$

4    $20{,}672$ $+ \;\; 3{\cdot}15\, Y_t$ $- \;\; 40{\cdot}41\, P_{t-2}$ $- \;\; 1090800\, BSM_{t-2}$ $+ \;\; 63181\, DP_t$
     $(5{\cdot}29)$ $(2{\cdot}17)$ $(0{\cdot}75)$ $(3{\cdot}49)$ $(2{\cdot}88)$

                           $- \;\; 1756{\cdot}40\, MR$ $- \;\; 2341{\cdot}79\, SR$ $+ \;\; 0{\cdot}74\, PC_{t-1}$
                               $(2{\cdot}77)$ $(3{\cdot}59)$ $(13{\cdot}78)$

     alpha $1 = - 0{\cdot}08$ $s = 1889$
           $(0{\cdot}51)$

5    $21{,}151$ $+ \;\; 4{\cdot}28\, Y_{t-2}$ $- \;\; 70{\cdot}49\, P_{t-2}$ $- \;\; 1133301\, BSM_{t-2}$ $+ \;\; 6512\, DP_t$
     $(5{\cdot}44)$ $(2{\cdot}33)$ $(1{\cdot}12)$ $(3{\cdot}61)$ $(3{\cdot}07)$

                           $- \;\; 1701{\cdot}30\, MR$ $- \;\; 2381{\cdot}89\, SR$ $+ \;\; 0{\cdot}72\, PC_{t-1}$
                               $(2{\cdot}67)$ $(3{\cdot}67)$ $(12{\cdot}94)$

     alpha $1 = - 0{\cdot}07$ $s = 1876$
           $(0{\cdot}45)$

---

demand is reduced through credit rationing is quite small — less than 2,500 units even when strong rationing is in effect. The importance of the flow of funds variable depends crucially on the length of lag on the flow of funds variable. FF_{t-2} in most formulations is not very significant (equation 3) and other lags are worse. Problems arise because of the inadequate specification of the time trend especially as the flow of funds has generally risen over the period. The lag is compatible with the estimated lag on the mortgage rate suggesting that changes in mortgage rates are closely related to changes in the flow of funds and that building societies do not react to variations immediately either by changing price or by rationing. The purchaser usually obtains a mortgage well before he actually buys and so is affected by even earlier rationing rules. Similarly he takes account of past income at the time of obtaining the mortgage (again the coefficient on lagged income although larger is not significantly different from income in the current period).

Table 6.8 shows what happens when population, stock and general price variables are included. When population, which is really only a trend term, is added the value of the constant term changes enormously because of the very large size of the population variable. More interestingly the explanatory value of the income variable is reduced so that it is no longer significantly different from zero. Both income and population however have the correct sign. This relationship reflects the trend nature of both income and population. FF_{t-3} now becomes the best estimate of the flow of funds and is significant at the 5 per cent level (equation 4) suggesting that once population is included as a trend term the real nature of the variation in the flow of funds is better able to make itself felt. When the general price level is introduced to give some idea of reaction to real rather than money changes (equation 5) the relative importance of house prices once again declines. The value of 's' is not reduced however and there is no reason to continue with this specification.

In some ways the results reported in Tables 6.7 and 6.8 suggest that as long as one trend term, such as income or population, is included the best estimates of short-term behaviour are obtained by not including other multicollinear trend terms. However there is a case for including stock and population in some cases in order to calculate useful elasticities. The evidence presented here suggests that the best equations for further analysis are those which include some measure of credit availability. When estimating two-staged least-squares we will concentrate particularly on equations 4 and 5 in Table 6.7 and equations 2 and 4 in Table 6.8, and any further analysis will be left until least-squares bias has been removed.

Table 6.8

Demand including population, stock and the general price level
Dependent variable = PC_t

(59 observations, seasonal and first quarter 1963 dummies included in all estimates)

---

1 $-245559 \cdot 64$ $+ 0 \cdot 25\, Y_t$ $- 125 \cdot 63\, P_{t-2}$ $- 869330\, BSM_{t-2}$ $- 50665\, DP_t$
      $(2 \cdot 57)$ $(0 \cdot 11)$ $(1 \cdot 80)$ $(2 \cdot 22)$ $(2 \cdot 66)$

                            $+ \quad 5 \cdot 71\, N_t$ $+ \quad 0 \cdot 57\, PC_{t-1}$
                                 $(2 \cdot 80)$ $(6 \cdot 31)$

           alpha 1 = $0 \cdot 16$ $s = 1924$
                 $(0 \cdot 92)$

2 -95740 $+ 1 \cdot 54\, Y_t$ $- \quad 69 \cdot 01\, P_{t-2}$ $- 960827\, BSM_{t-2}$ $+ 60255\, DP_t$
      $(1 \cdot 01)$ $(0 \cdot 77)$ $(1 \cdot 15)$ $(2 \cdot 83)$ $(2 \cdot 83)$

            $+ \; 0 \cdot 67\, PC_{t-1}$ $- 1265 \cdot 82\, MR$ $- 1812 \cdot 24\, SR$ $+ \quad 2 \cdot 50\, N_t$
            $(8 \cdot 49)$ $(1 \cdot 68)$ $(2 \cdot 31)$ $(1 \cdot 22)$

           alpha 1 = $-0 \cdot 03$ $s = 1879$
                 $(0 \cdot 19)$

3 $-261662 \cdot 16$ $+ 1 \cdot 11\, Y_t$ $- 125 \cdot 78\, P_{t-2}$ $- 773420\, BSM_{t-2}$ $+ 49896\, DP$
      $(2 \cdot 48)$ $(0 \cdot 40)$ $(1 \cdot 72)$ $(1 \cdot 74)$ $(2 \cdot 65)$

                     $+ \quad 6 \cdot 86\, N_t$ $- \quad 2 \cdot 94\, ST_{t-1}$ $+ \quad 0 \cdot 55\, PC_{t-1}$
                     $(2 \cdot 14)$ $(0 \cdot 48)$ $(5 \cdot 55)$

           alpha 1 = $0 \cdot 20$ $s = 1940$
                 $(1 \cdot 01)$

4 $-297450 \cdot 49$ $+ 0 \cdot 48\, Y_t$ $- 156 \cdot 33\, P_{t-2}$ $- 558851\, BSM_{t-2}$ $+ 50437\, DP$
      $(3 \cdot 24)$ $(0 \cdot 19)$ $(2 \cdot 40)$ $(1 \cdot 35)$ $(2 \cdot 63)$

                     $+ \quad 18 \cdot 00\, FF_{t-3}-$ $4 \cdot 10\, ST_{t-1}$ $+ \quad 7 \cdot 97\, N_t$
                     $(2 \cdot 32)$ $(0 \cdot 79)$ $(2 \cdot 99)$

           alpha 1 = $0 \cdot 10$ $s = 1858$
                 $(0 \cdot 55)$

5 $68380 \cdot 76$ $+ 15 \cdot 50\, Y_{t-2}$ $- \quad 89 \cdot 18\, P_{t-2}$ $- 738658\, BSM_{t-2}$ $+ 48818\, DP$
      $(4 \cdot 76)$ $(4 \cdot 16)$ $(1 \cdot 07)$ $(1 \cdot 79)$ $(2 \cdot 88)$

                     $+ \quad 10 \cdot 08\, FF_{t-3}-$ $883 \cdot 88\, RPI_t$ $+ \quad 0 \cdot 47\, PC_{t-1}$
                     $(1 \cdot 26)$ $(3 \cdot 37)$ $(4 \cdot 86)$

           alpha 1 = $0 \cdot 30$ $s = 1864$
                 $(1 \cdot 80)$

Notes

[1] The total quantity of new accommodation units is made up of net conversions and new completions. There are no quarterly estimates of conversions available and rather than use demolitions alone net increases from existing stock have been disregarded in the model.

[2] Symbols are given in Appendix A.

[3] The problems of assessing household formation and forecasting its relationship to the demand for housing are discussed in A.E. Holmans 'A Forecast of Effective Demand for Housing in Great Britain in the 1970s', *Social Trends* vol. 1, 1970.

[4] S.J. Maisel, 'Changes in the Rate and Components of Household Formation', *Journal of the American Statistical Association*, June 1960, suggests that as equilibrium in the housing market is reached there may be a significant structural upward movement in the number of separate households. This happened in the United States in the late 1950s and early 1960s.

[5] The 'headship' rate is the proportion of any group (defined often in terms of age, sex and marital status) who are heads of households. They tend to be fairly constant within a given adult population and only change slowly over time. See e.g. L. Winnick, *American Housing and its Use* Wiley, New York 1957, chap.8; J.B. Cullingworth, *Housing Needs and Planning Policy,* Routledge & Kegen Paul, London 1960, chap. 9, and S.J. Maisel, (op.cit). In the UK the fall in family size, the growing number of old people and more and earlier marriages have increased the number of one and two-person households and decreased large households but 'headship rates' within each of these groups have increased very little.

[6] M.G. Reid, *Housing and Income*, University of Chicago Press, Chicago, and R.F. Muth, 'The Demand for Non-Farm Housing' in A.C. Houthakker, (ed.), *The Demand for Durable Goods*, University of Chicago Press, Chicago 1960.

[7] It would be possible to use the Friedman estimates of personal income weights — as was done by Reid, (op.cit.) Muth (op.cit.), and T.H. Lee, 'Demand for Housing: A Cross Section Analysis', *Review of Economics and Statistics*, vol. 45, no. 2, 1963. These can be found in M. Friedman *A Theory of the Consumption Function* Princeton University Press, Princeton 1957. The main objection to following this method is that it requires nine extra quarters' data — which would reduce the calculable period for the regression analysis considerably. Further there is no reason to believe that behaviour patterns are constant between countries.

[8] Substitution to other tenures assumes that an equilibrium tenure

split existed before the price rise. To the extent that entry into owner-occupation is constrained by non-market factors it may be that those already in this sector obtain surplus utility over market price. A small change in price will not therefore cause a shift into another tenure. Moreover, the real price rise may be less than the apparent rise, because the implicit subsidy to owner-occupation is related to price as well as to income. These constraints have been examined in more detail in the first section.

[9] Most building societies lend only to the creditworthy and on good quality housing. Thus a price index based on mortgages will be biased because the proportion of good quality, relatively expensive housing sold will be too great. The Nationwide Building Society has probably the most open mortgage policy and thus their figures should be less biased than the other building societies.

[10] This index takes no account of changes in the tax rebate of interest payments which also affects the real price paid. It thus makes the over-simple assumption that the implicit subsidy remains constant over the period of estimation.

[11] The formal analysis of the effect of expectations can be found in the general inflation literature. The limiting case is analysed by M. Friedman, 'The Role of Monetary Policy', *American Economic Review*, vol. LVIII, No. 1, 1968, and discussed in detail by R.M. Solow, *Price Expectations and the Behaviour of the Price Level*, Manchester University Press, Manchester, 1969. It states that if the expected inflation rate is solely a function of current and past price increases, then any rate of inflation and therefore of increase in house prices is sustainable. This can be stated as:

$$P_{t+1}^* - P_t^* = \theta \ (P_t - P_t^*) \qquad 0 < \theta < 1$$

where P is the proportional rate of change of the price level, P^* is the expected rate of inflation and θ is the weight attached to earlier rates of inflation. P_{t+1}^* is therefore the weighted average of P_t, P_{t-1}, P_{t-2} etc. with geometrically decaying weights which add to one in a short period if θ is close to one and over a long period if θ is close to zero (i.e. θ depends on the speed of learning). If the actual rate of inflation remains constant the expected rate will move towards the constant actual rate and at the limit will equal it.

We may include in the model the effects of real economic variables on price by the modification that:

$$P = f(x) + P^*$$

where $f(x)$ stands for a set of real characteristics. This would lead to differences between the actual and the expected rate of inflation except where $f(x)$ is equal to zero. Such analysis suggests that in the absence of any other economic variables any rate of change of house prices could be sustainable through expectations which feed on themselves. This is unlikely to be fully realised in the housing market where there are many real constraints particularly in finance. These other, real, factors involved are more important in a particular sector than in the economy as a whole, because of the ability to substitute other goods and investments. However, the relative ease of access to finance for housing in comparison to other investments may offset some of the restraining economic factors and at the worst may lead to ever increasing house price rises. Prices continue to rise from the increased desire to hedge against inflation and increase the incentive to hedge. Yet many people can obtain finance only to bring forward housing expenditure. This is because property provides its own security and the finance market for housing is relatively well developed in comparison to that for other sectors. As hedging itself puts up prices and the demand to hedge is greatest in the housing market because of financial constraints elsewhere, the price goes up most rapidly in this sector. If expectations are based on the current situation in this sector rather than in the economy as a whole the greater rate of increases here will feed itself to be curtailed only when financing becomes impossible or when expectations themselves change as a result of a structural change in the effect of other economic variables.

[12] See the discussion in section one. In particular C. St. J., O'Herlihy, J.E. Spencer, 'Building Societies' Behaviour 1955 — 1970', *National Institute Economic Review,* no. 61, 1972, have examined building society behaviour in the UK G. Fromm, 'Econometric Models of the Residential Construction Sector: A Comparison Paper', presented at the Housing Model Conference for Federal Home Loans Bank Board, Washington DC, 1971, surveys the relevant literature for the United States.

[13] This will normally be most important for first time purchasers who generally borrow up to their limit. Yet, first purchasers are less likely to buy a new house, and therefore the new housing market is perhaps not so directly affected by the building societies because they favour new houses. However, the market will be indirectly affected because most purchasers of new houses must sell their existing property and their ability to find a buyer will be affected by the stringency of building society rules.

[14] Building societies may also vary the proportion of the valuation of the house that they are prepared to finance or even increase valuation levels more slowly than house prices. Both of these measures increase the importance of non-price constraints.

[15] This may be offset for individuals with an outstanding mortgage by extending the repayment period but such an increase directly affects any new purchase of a house. Mortgages are negotiated at the time of sale and cannot be transferred.

[16] C.St.J. O'Herlihy and J.E. Spencer, op.cit.

[17] See L.R. Klein, *Textbook of Econometrics,* Row Petersen & Co., Evanston 1956, p. 314, for a discussion of the use of dummies with quarterly data. For a general discussion of dummy variables in regression equations, see D. Suits, 'Use of Dummy Variables in Regression Equations', *Journal of American Statistical Association,* no. 52, 1967.

[18] See M. Nerlove, and K.F. Wallis, 'The Durbin-Watson Statistic in Inappropriate Situations', *Econometrica* vol.34, No. 1, 1966, for a discussion of the difficulties of interpreting the estimate of autocorrelation under these conditions.

[19] Two programmes which enable this to be done have been developed by David Hendry at the London School of Economics. Rth Order Autoregressive Least Squares (RALS) was used for determining the order of the auto-correlation. This allows one to test for all orders of auto-correlation up to seventh order both separately and together. General Instrumental Variable Estimation (GIVE) was used for all later estimation because it is more flexible once the order of autocorrelation is determined and only a single order was found to be significant.

[20] GIVE unlike RALS can be used later for two-staged least-squares estimation and possibly also for forecasting purposes.

7 The Supply of New Houses

Next we discuss possible structures of the supply of starts equation, the data available for testing the hypotheses put forward about its structure and the single-staged least-squares estimates which determine the choice of equation for the final model.

7.1 Supply: statistical analysis

The supply of accommodation in the UK is made up of the stock of existing houses, plus completions and increases via conversions less demolitions. We have decided to concentrate in our statistical analysis entirely on the supply of new private dwellings that is simply completions.

Many of the hypotheses about new supply are extremely difficult to test because of lack of data. It has been suggested for instance, that new supply depends upon builders' profits, availability of credit to builders, and the time taken to sell completed houses. Yet adequate statistical information to test this simple hypothesis is not available. Data for the first two variables can be obtained but information about the period that a completed (or near-completed) house on average remains unsold is not available in time-series form.[1] Another suggestion is that vacancy rates of existing houses could be used to give some estimate for builders' expectations of future profits[2] but no time-series data is available in Great Britain except that provided through rating returns. This is not sensitive to variations because one can only assess the loss in revenue from vacancies in a whole rating area. The data also does not exist in quarterly form. Because of the paucity of relevant data this type of variable has been excluded from the supply equation. We can however attempt to quantify the effects of profits, costs and financial constraints on the supply of starts.

If house prices increase relative to other prices, and costs remain the same, there is an incentive for builders to expand their production of houses. The builder may also substitute speculative house building for local authority housing contracts or for other types of construction. In order to make these decisions the builder wishes to predict future prices rather than look at current relationships because some months will pass before he succeeds in obtaining planning permission, putting in the infra-

105

structure, designing and actually completing the house. The decision to produce is therefore dependent not just on current prices but on the expectations of future house price changes. An increase or the expectation of an increase in house prices will *ceteris paribus* increase supply. We therefore expect that an important independent variable in the supply equation will be the price of new dwellings (although in theory we would expect the relationship to be modified by any changes in the timing of sales relative to completions). The same house price index that was used in the demand equation produced by the Nationwide Building Society can be used in the supply equation, reflecting the actual price received by the speculative builder.

But profits are a function not just of price but of costs. These are made up of wages, building materials, finance and land costs. They do not all vary independently of the behaviour of house prices. In particular the price of land is mainly demand determined because of supply inelasticities and so when builders wish to expand production the price of land increases. The more inelastic the supply of land the more a given change in demand will increase the price. Although taking the country as a whole there is a great deal of land available, the quantity is very limited in or near urban centres and is further reduced by local authority controls on planning permission. Because of these it is not normally possible to substitute housing for other land uses and it may even be difficult to vary the intensity of use. Supply in a particular area at a given time is likely to be almost completely inelastic.

The quantity of land which could be made available may be further reduced by landowners' own expectations. If they believe that in the future land prices are going to rise faster than other prices their expected rate of return on holding land is greater than the return they can obtain by selling and investing elsewhere. They will, therefore, have an incentive to hold the land off the market and so shift the whole supply curve.[3] This expectational effect makes the builder's position more difficult. If he holds a land bank he is in the landowner's position and would do better to keep his land stock rather than to build because he expects prices to rise further in the future. If he holds no land his profit from increased demand disappears in higher land costs. At the limit builders bidding against each other for the available land will be prepared to force up prices to a level which leaves them only normal profit and thus the whole house price increase is passed on to the landowner. Builders' incentives to expand housing construction following house price increases will be reduced, if not completely removed, by the resulting increase in land prices. Such an hypothesis has important policy implications but depends on the nature

106

of the supply elasticity. It is extremely difficult to obtain land price information to test the hypothesis because very little time-series data on land prices exist. Where information is available averages hide enormous differences between regions and between conubations. This makes the figures rather meaningless, even though we are directly interested in national behaviour.

Because the land price index published by the Department of the Environment runs only from 1963 and is published at six-monthly intervals the information could not be included in our quarterly model. A surrogate which assumed that land costs are 20 per cent of total building costs and that its price has risen at a constant rate of 2 per cent per quarter was used instead. This does reflect general trends in the earlier period but becomes more unsatisfactory in the late 1960s and the early 1970s.

There are adequate series for both building materials and wage rates published in the *Monthly Digest of Statistics* but the proportion of each which makes up total construction costs is a matter of informed guesswork. Discussions at the Building Research Establishment suggested that a figure of 20 per cent building materials, 60 per cent wages and 20 per cent land are not far from reality and the construction cost index was calculated on this basis. Another difficulty which arises is that the use of wage rates in this way assumes constant labour productivity, an assumption which is likely to bias costs upwards over the period of estimation. Although attempts have been made to assess changes in productivity there is no adequate time-series measure and so the bias cannot be removed.[4]

The other important constituents of costs are those relating to finance. Most builders have little capital of their own and are dependent on banks for finance, use their land as collateral and often have to borrow even to buy this. They are therefore regarded as poor risks by banks and face high interest charges. Increases in general rates of interest are likely to increase builders' costs immediately and by larger than average amounts. Squeezes make building impossible because of builders' inability to obtain funds.

There are two effects to be examined: the effect that changes in the rate of interest have on builders' desires to start new dwellings and the effect of the availability of credit in constraining this desire.

In some equations the long-term rate of interest on consols was taken to represent both the rate of interest that builders had to pay on borrowed money, and to act as a surrogate for the availability of credit, which it is hypothesised is fairly rapidly reflected in changes in this rate. This is a simplification of the actual situation, but government policy since 1954 has been such that rates of interest have generally increased at the same time as availability has declined and so the two aspects are closely related.

107

Another possible hypothesis is that the effect of changes in availability might well be very strong in comparison to those of the cost of credit and affect starts in a different way. In some formulations therefore cost and availability were included separately. This possibility is regarded as important because of the generally held view that the timing of new building is directly affected by the ability of builders to borrow from the banks. The reasons for this view are discussed in detail in chapters 1 − 3 and the specifications examined in this chapter attempt to test these hypotheses to some extent.

One possible way of including availability separately from cost would be to construct dummies in the same way as those used in the demand equation. As an approximation the actual demand dummies were used although these are meant to reflect specifically the availability of mortgage finance. There may be good reasons for including these particular dummies, or indeed the net flow of funds to building societies in that builders build on speculation and have high financing costs of holding and are therefore strongly affected by the state of demand. If they expect credit controls to sqeeze building societies' funds and thus reduce effective demand they will expect profits to be cut either because of price cuts or because of increases in holding costs. They will then cut back on production accordingly even though they are themselves able to obtain finance. As few costs are attached to not building, builders are likely to be conservative decision-makers and cut-back whenever they see difficulties ahead. On the other hand, starting up again may be financially difficult because of the need to buy land and time consuming because of the problems of obtaining planning permission and the time required to actually complete a house. Thus credit availability for purchasers may be almost as important in determining starts as the cost and availability of finance to suppliers themselves.

A number of other variables which reflect the state of the economy and expectations relating to prices were also included in some formulations and will be discussed when we examine specific results.

Starts in the previous quarter were included in some specifications partially to reflect the idea that builders' expectations about the future are based on past behaviour. Also in some measure such a variable might reflect the capacity of the industry. Its sign is therefore ambiguous. In most formulations a linear trend was also included. The seasonal dummies used were the same as for completions, and a dummy for the first quarter of 1963, when bad weather prevented most construction activity, was also included.

7.2   Statistical estimation – supply

Estimation of the supply equation was carried out in the same way as for demand. First those specifications which reflected the economic hypotheses were estimated by single-stage least-squares methods although it is recognised that this method introduces bias into the estimation procedure. On the other hand it does provide a simple way of examining a range of possible variations. Next modifications were made on the basis of these results. The best equations were then chosen to form part of the full model to be estimated by two-staged least-squares. The model is then used to analyse the market and its reactions to changes in the economic variables.

Table 7.1 sets out the first estimates which were computed using ordinary least-squares techniques. Although however specified the effect of the rate of interest is always negative and significant, the most effective form is when the variable is lagged by one quarter. The signs on the other main explanatory variables, construction costs and price, are not always correct, and the coefficients are extremely variable. When a trend term is introduced to reflect the general increase in the number of starts a correct sign on costs is obtained but the sign on price is then incorrect (equations 2 and 3).Costs are defined in such a way that a trend term is included via land costs and the variable is multicollinear with the term trend. Modifications to include longer lags on construction costs and price do not increase the explanatory value, nor does redefining cost and price so that they enter in real terms (CR, PR: equation 4). The main reason for poor results is the bias resulting from autocorrelation. The Durbin-Watson statistics certainly suggest very large autocorrelation. So rather than try more complex formulations of the supply equation it was decided to remove the bias first.

Tests to remove autocorrelation up to seventh order using RALS showed that there was no significant autocorrelation greater than first-order but that alpha 1, the coefficient of first-order autocorrelation, was often as high as 0·85 with a 't' value of more than 13. The hypothesised equations were therefore re-estimated to exclude first-order autocorrelation. Table 7.2 shows the results when GIVE was used to make these re-estimations. In each case the alpha 1 value is given to show the extent of first-order autocorrelation that has been removed. The results now reflect our hypotheses fairly closely and suggest that the supply equation is reasonably well specified, except in respect of the poor cost data.

' The coefficient on the rate of interest is not greatly affected by the removal of first-order autocorrelation. It is still always significant at the

109

Table 7.1

The supply of starts
Dependent variable PS_t

(61 observations, seasonal and first quarter 1963 dummies included in all equations)

No.	Constant						Statistics
1	35097 (3·41)	− 9847·74 r_{t-1} (−4·28)	+ 283·84 CC_t (1·00)	+ 197·93 P_t (1·13)			$\bar{r}^2 = 0.51$ $DW = 0.36$.
2	107976·21 (9·87)	− 5383·86 r_t (−3·50)	− 515·419 CC_t (−2·50)	+ 188·66 P_t (−1·53)	+ 1924·68 T (8·69)		$\bar{r}^2 = 0.79$ $DW = 0.86$.
3	110009·53 (11·54)	− 7238·81 r_{t-1} (−5·28)	− 424·82 CC_t (−2·36)	− 218·26 P_t (−1·98)	+ 1959·68 T (10·14)		$\bar{r}^2 = 0.83$ $DW = 0.94$
4	60859·71 (4·35)	− 4755·86 r_{t-1} (−3·62)	− 151·42 CC_t (−0·90)	− 200·48 P_t (2·10)	+ 1181·58 T (4·82)	+ 0·43 PS_{t-1} (4·34)	$\bar{r}^2 = 0.87$ $DW = 1.76$.
5	14553·90 (0·32)	− 5631·02 r_{t-1} (−4·30)	+ 44711·22 CC/R_{t-1} (1·08)	− 30512 P/R_{t-1} (−2·51)	+ 614·17 T (2·51)	+ 0·55 PS_{t-1} (5·88)	$\bar{r}^2 = 0.87$ $DW = 1.84$.

5 per cent level and is most significant when lagged one period (Table 7.2, equation 1). This presumably reflects the planning time between the builders obtaining finance and actually starting work on the dwelling.

The signs on the cost and price variables are as hypothesised once the autocorrelation is removed. Their coefficients are significant (Table 7.2, equation 1 and 2). The best results are obtained using monetary indices for both costs and prices. When values deflated by the general price level are used instead (CR, PR) the coefficient on price is marginally more significant but that on costs becomes insignificant, (Table 7.2, equation 5). This result probably reflects the poor economic basis of the cost index in which there is no true land cost information and no adjustment made for productivity changes. On the other hand we could postulate that the builder faces a borrowing constraint determined in absolute values but that his objective is defined in terms of the real value of the price obtained. This is examined in Table 7.2, equation 4. There is very slightly more explanatory value than when both are deflated but the difference is not significant. On the basis of these results we cannot rule out the use of variables in money or real terms.

If lagged values of the independent variables are used instead of the coefficients on current ones both variables become insignificant. Explanatory value is reduced. An example is given in Table 7.2, equation 3.

In some versions starts lagged one period were included to reflect the level of capacity and general trends in finance and supply. Before autocorrelation was removed the variable was very significant. Once removed it is totally insignificant in all estimated versions (e.g. Table 7.2, equation 2). This suggests that its earlier significance was entirely the result of misspecification of the autocorrelation present in the original version. Once autocorrelation is removed we can regard starts in a given period as independent of starts in earlier periods.

We thus have a supply of starts equation which depends on rational economic variables, i.e. the costs of production including financial costs and the price of the good being produced. We now examine a number of possible complexities resulting from the special nature of housing finance, and from variations in the economic climate.

Builders are very much affected by financial constraints because they depend for working capital on short-term finance borrowed from the banks. If this capital is bound up in completed dwellings they may find it difficult to borrow further in order to continue work-in-progress. We might therefore expect building societies' credit rationing behaviour to affect supply because this helps to determine the ease of sale. As credit gets tighter, speculative builders predict restricted demand and a longer

Table 7.2

Supply of starts – autocorrelation removed
Dependent variable PS_t

(59 observations, seasonal and first quarter 1963 dummies included in all equations)

1	67628·71 (4·05)	−	5312·85 r_{t-1} (2·75)	−	576·88 CC_t (2·25)	+	619·53 P_t (3·11)	Ds		
	Alpha 1 = 0·86 (13·12)	$s = 3696·18$								
2	81940·52 (5·05)	−	5589·84 r_{t-1} (2·83)	−	592·60 CC_t (2·25)	+	625·07 P_t (3·09)	−	0·01 PS_{t-1} (0·11)	+ Ds
	Alpha 1 = 0·83 (10·56)	$s = 3724·96$								
3	−20394·83 (0·47)	−	4961·67 r_{t-1} (2·44)	+	76932·90 CR_{t-2} (1·66)	+	11649·75 PR_{t-1} (0·51)	+ Ds		
	Alpha 1 = 0·78 (7·71)	$s = 3980·85$								
4	−4438·02 (0·22)	−	3704·10 r_{t-1} (2·04)	−	194·15 CC_t (1·28)	+	79192·71 PR_t (3·47)	+ Ds		
	Alpha 1 = 0·81 (10·27)	$s = 3637·43$								
5	22518·61 (0·63)	−	4956·74 r_{t-1} (3·01)	−	29300·71 CR_t (0·76)	+	70164·23 PR_t (3·23)	+ Ds		
	Alpha 1 = 0·82 (10·85)	$s = 3678·13$								

waiting time between completion and sale. If this is how builders behave the demand credit availability variables should be significant in determining the supply of starts. Table 7.3, equation 1, tests this hypothesis by including the flow of funds lagged by two periods. In all formulations the coefficient is significant and is not greatly affected by which specification of the full equation is being tested. This suggests that there is little multicollinearity between the flow of funds and other variables. The only effect on the other independent variables is to reduce slightly the size of the coefficient on the rate of interest. This is predictable because the flow of funds into building societies is related not only to the likely ease of obtaining credit for house purchase but also to the general availability of credit in the economy as a whole, which in turn helps determine the rate of interest. The availability and cost of credit to housing suppliers are not therefore fully separable variables. Other possible lags on the flow of funds were tested. The current value, or a one-period lag, produced insignificant results. The coefficients on three or four-period lags were also considerably less significant than that on the two-period lag.

If the dummies devised by O'Herlihy and Spencer are included instead of the flow of funds, the significance of the rate of interest declines as before, but the coefficients on the dummies themselves are not significant (Table 7.3, equation 4). This result, in comparison with the significance of the flow of funds suggests that builders look at the reality of available demand credit rather than at any secondary discussions of the state of future credit. The insignificance of the dummy variables also implies that if the O'Herlihy-Spencer dummies correctly reflect demand finance availability, credit rationing to builders is determined differently from that to house purchasers. This may possibly be because credit restrictions to builders start earlier and ease later than to the rest of the economy over the economic cycle.

When using either the flow of funds or availability dummies we are not truly separating the hypothesis of builders' taking account of demand expectations from that which assumes they are directly affected by credit rationing. Unhappily there is no data available to test credit rationing to supply directly. The considerable significance of the rate of interest in all formulations suggests that building firms are greatly affected by the cost of credit and perhaps that cost and availability are very strongly correlated on the supply side. The length of lag on the flow of funds might also imply that it is a surrogate for a demand rather than a supply constraint.

We have found that the rate of inflation is an important determinant of demand because of the nature of housing as a capital asset. On the supply side there are less likely to be strong effects for builders are only involved

Table 7.3

The effects of the availability of credit
Dependent variable PS_t

(59 observations, seasonal and first quarter 1963 dummies included in all equations)

1 $\quad$ $79450 \cdot 84$ $\quad$ $- 4872 \cdot 99\, r_{t-1}$ $\quad$ $- 682 \cdot 30\, CC_t$ $\quad$ $+ 591 \cdot 50\, P_t$ $\quad$ $+ 37 \cdot 35\, FF_{t-2}$ $\quad$ $+ Ds$
$\quad\quad$ $(4 \cdot 60)$ $\qquad$ $(2 \cdot 65)$ $\qquad\quad$ $(2 \cdot 78)$ $\qquad\quad$ $(3 \cdot 10)$ $\qquad\quad$ $(2 \cdot 66)$

Alpha $1 = 0 \cdot 87 \quad s = 3489 \cdot 68$
$\quad\quad$ $(14 \cdot 29)$

2 $\quad$ $8948 \cdot 57$ $\quad$ $- 3291 \cdot 98\, r_{t-1}$ $\quad$ $- 322 \cdot 67\, CC_t$ $\quad$ $+ 77290 \cdot 31\, PR_t$ $\quad$ $+ 37 \cdot 65\, FF_{t-2}$ $\quad$ $+ Ds$
$\quad\quad$ $(0 \cdot 46)$ $\qquad$ $(1 \cdot 92)$ $\qquad\quad$ $(2 \cdot 14)$ $\qquad\quad$ $(3 \cdot 50)$ $\qquad\quad$ $(2 \cdot 70)$

Alpha $1 = 0 \cdot 83 \quad s = 3429 \cdot 50$
$\quad\quad$ $(11 \cdot 44)$

3 $\quad$ $67702 \cdot 98$ $\quad$ $- 5671 \cdot 14\, r_{t-1}$ $\quad$ $- 53445 \cdot 35\, CR_t$ $\quad$ $+ 66002 \cdot 71\, PR_t$ $\quad$ $+ 31 \cdot 46\, FF_{t-2}$ $\quad$ $+ Ds$
$\quad\quad$ $(1 \cdot 86)$ $\qquad$ $(3 \cdot 59)$ $\qquad\quad$ $(1 \cdot 38)$ $\qquad\quad$ $(3 \cdot 09)$ $\qquad\quad$ $(2 \cdot 21)$

Alpha $1 = 0 \cdot 81 \quad s = 3515 \cdot 43$
$\quad\quad$ $(10 \cdot 77)$

4 $\quad$ $69660 \cdot 50$ $\quad$ $- 4690 \cdot 13\, r_{t-1}$ $\quad$ $- 640 \cdot 68\, CC_t$ $\quad$ $+ 648 \cdot 24\, P_t$ $\quad$ $- 1422 \cdot 13\, MR$ $\quad$ $- 3051 \cdot 43\, SR$ $\quad$ $+ Ds$
$\quad\quad$ $(4 \cdot 14)$ $\qquad$ $(2 \cdot 40)$ $\qquad\quad$ $(2 \cdot 47)$ $\qquad\quad$ $(3 \cdot 25)$ $\qquad\quad$ $(0 \cdot 98)$ $\qquad\quad$ $(1 \cdot 58)$

Alpha $1 = 0 \cdot 86 \quad s = 3672 \cdot 78$
$\quad\quad$ $(12 \cdot 82)$

5 $\quad$ $80750 \cdot 43$ $\quad$ $- 5256 \cdot 07\, r_{t-1}$ $\quad$ $- 594 \cdot 04\, CC_t$ $\quad$ $+ 622 \cdot 14\, P_t$ $\quad$ $- 60144 \cdot 94\, DW$ $\quad$ $+ Ds$
$\quad\quad$ $(5 \cdot 33)$ $\qquad$ $(2 \cdot 68)$ $\qquad\quad$ $(2 \cdot 31)$ $\qquad\quad$ $(3 \cdot 14)$ $\qquad\quad$ $(1 \cdot 00)$

Alpha $1 = 0 \cdot 83 \quad s = 3686 \cdot 71$
$\quad\quad$ $(11 \cdot 81)$

6 $\quad$ $79296 \cdot 25$ $\quad$ $- 5423 \cdot 72\, r_{t-1}$ $\quad$ $- 535 \cdot 88\, CC_t$ $\quad$ $+ 575 \cdot 14\, P_t$ $\quad$ $+ 16278 \cdot 55\, DP_t$ $\quad$ $+ Ds$
$\quad\quad$ $(5 \cdot 16)$ $\qquad$ $(2 \cdot 75)$ $\qquad\quad$ $(1 \cdot 93)$ $\qquad\quad$ $(2 \cdot 64)$ $\qquad\quad$ $(0 \cdot 56)$

Alpha $1 = 0 \cdot 82 \quad s = 3713 \cdot 40$
$\quad\quad$ $(11 \cdot 47)$

114

in fairly short-term decisions. The most important effect of inflation on supply might well be that changes in the rate of inflation result in sanctions of monetary controls which affect supply as discussed above. To test for direct effects of inflation we included the rate of change of general prices (Table 7.3, equation 5). It was almost entirely insignificant. The coefficient was also not significantly different from zero when the rate of change of house prices rather than general prices was used (Table 7.3, equation 6). House price increases do not appear to cause builders to desire to build more houses. This result upholds the hypothesis that builders' profits do not increase greatly when house prices go up presumably either because land prices increase as well or because of expectations of future credit difficulties. The numerous possibilities are difficult to separate and test adequately without further information about land costs, alternative investment opportunities for builders and a more precise variable to reflect credit availability to housing construction.

The tested supply equations reflect the costs of production, including financial costs, the current price of new houses and usually include an availability variable to represent the expected ease of sale. No direct account is taken of the rate of inflation. Although we have not produced a very sophisticated supply structure the versions in Table 7.3 (especially equations 1 and 2) are based on simple economic theory and have significant coefficients. Undoubtedly the most worrying aspect is the large constant term which may cause difficulties in the full model, especially in relation to forecasting. We examine this problem in more detail when we come to assess the full model in section three.

Notes

[1] It is sometimes possible to obtain a general impression of the waiting time between completion and sale from the *Estates Gazette* and also indirectly from estate agents returns to the Department of the Environment but neither of these are in numerical form.

[2] This aspect of the housing market has been stressed by many American authors. In the USA vacancy rates are considerably higher and more variable than in the UK (HUD estimates up to 10 per cent vacancy rates by 1975 — see *U.S. Congress First Annual Report on National Housing Goals*, US Government Printing Office, Washington 1969. This variation in vacancy rates can be used to measure the extent of excess demand in disequilibrium models. In more simple models it can be used as a measure of builders' expectations. See e.g. S.J. Maisel, 'Fluctuations in

Residential Construction Starts' *American Economic Review*, June 1963, and earlier works by V.L. Bassie, *Economic Forecasting*, McGraw-Hill, New York 1958, Appendix C; C. Rapkin, L. Winnick, and D.M. Blank, *Housing Market Analysis*, US Housing and Home Finance Agency, Washington 1953.

³ This point is made very clearly in R.V. Turvey, *The Economics of Real Property*, Allen & Unwin, London 1957.

⁴ See e.g. National Board for Prices and Incomes *Pay and Conditions in the Building Industry Report No. 92,* Cmnd 3837, HMSO, London 1968, which discusses the difficulties of measuring productivity given the apparently varying numbers in the work force. These vary mainly because of changes in the taxation structure which produce a 'lump' of self-employed, said to vary greatly in size from year to year. Some work on productivity at the building site level has also been done at the Building Research Establishment e.g. W.S. Forbes, 'A Survey of Progress in House Building', Building Research Station Current Paper 25/69 (unpublished but available on request).

8 The Relationship between Starts and Completions

So far two equations have been examined in detail, the demand for completions equation and the supply of starts equation. It is now necessary to link these two. An increase in demand, which results in an increase in price, cannot be met by an immediate expansion of the housing stock because it takes time to build houses and because there may also be lags in suppliers' reactions. We need to know therefore how the desire of builders to provide new houses reflected in starts is related to actual new completions, i.e. how rapidly starts are completed and the shape of the adjustment process. It would be expected that the general structure would be of the form $C_t^s = (S_{t-1} \ldots S_{t-n})$ but the shape of the distributed lag must be determined. The simplest type of lag structure would be that suggested by Koyck[1] who fits an exponential function where the speed of adjustment is proportional to the distance from equilibrium. Institutional and technological factors mean that it is difficult for a house to be completed within three months — and it will usually take longer. If the adjustment were to be similar to a Koyck distributed lag one would expect a large proportion of the adjustment to take place perhaps as late as the third quarter, with smaller and smaller coefficients for each further quarter until the adjustments were complete.

Another possible formulation is the lag structure suggested by Almon.[2] This requires that we specify the shape and the length of the lag before estimation. In order to determine the end point constraints and the degree of the curve we require information from past experience or from analysis of the theoretical possibilities and available data. Estimates of the 't' ratios determining the significance of the Almon lags are biased upwards because these extra constraints are not forced to reduce the degrees of freedom. A number of articles have now appeared querying the use of the Almon lag on theoretical grounds. In particular, Schmidt and Waud[3] have shown how sensitive the technique is to the choice of length of lag. As we have little ex-ante information on which to base the choice of the required restrictions we reject the use of the Almon lags. In such circumstances it is better to use a less specific type of lag such as that suggested by Jorgenson which allows the lag structure to take any shape.[4]

One problem which relates to all simple distributed lag structures is that they assume the time form to be fixed over the period of estimation. This assumption is made here although there has been variation in the average time lag between start and completion over the period. The Department of the Environment publishes estimates of the time lag between starts and completions on the basis of first in, first out, and these show (see Table 8.1) a general increase in the construction time over the period involved. The bias in estimating the shape of the distributed lag resulting from these variations is not as great as at first might be imagined because the model is a quarterly one and the variations in the average time of building in the private sector are rarely more than a quarter. It may,

Table 8.1

Estimated time lag: start to completion (months),
Great Britain (all dwellings)

	Public sector*	Private sector
1957*	12·6	8·5
1958	12·7	8·4
1959	12·8	8·0
1960	13·8	8·3
1961	14·8	8·8
1962	15·1	9·6
1963	15·5	10·4
1964	15·0	9·9
1965	16·2	10·9
1966	16·3 (15·8)	12·0
1967	15·3	12·0
1968	15·1	12·3
1969	16·3	13·0
1970	16·7	13·6
1971	16·8	12·0
1972	17·7	11·4

* The lag is longer in the public sector mainly because project size is normally larger. It also varies with changes in the proportion of flats to houses.

Sources: *Housing and Construction Statistics,* each issue.

however, somewhat affect the value and significance of individual coefficients.[5]

Any variation in the time lag between start and completion could be part of another explanation based on the waiting-time hypothesis. This suggests that suppliers react to changes in the business cycle, length of order books, etc. by expanding or contracting the period of production.[6] If this were so the distributed lag would not be fixed over the estimation period but would vary with the economic cycle. It would then be necessary to build further economic variables into the equation. These variables would be of a similar type to those already included in the starts and completions equations and there might well be identification and estimation difficulties. In the current model we have excluded this possibility and calculate a fixed distributed lag using initially Jorgenson's formulation. Our results are only a first attempt. It is certainly an area in which considerable further work should be concentrated.

The model we estimate here implies that suppliers wish to supply completed dwellings but that there must be a time lag between start and completion for both technical and economic reasons. This can be described by a distributed lag either in the form:

$$\text{(a)} \quad C_t^s = f\,(S_{t-i} \ldots S_{t-n})$$

or, as in the demand equation, by the equation

$$\text{(b)} \quad C_t^s - C_{t-1}^s = f(S_{t-i} \ldots S_{t-n})$$

which can be estimated as:

$$C_t^s = g(S_{t-i} \ldots S_{t-n}, C_{t-i}).$$

In (a) we are assuming that all starts reach completion in $n+1$ periods while in (b) we assume an infinite lag. It is possible that the inclusion of C_{t-1} in (b) may simply pick up any misspecification of the autoregressive error and this could cause difficulties when we systematically attempt to remove any autoregression errors.

Earlier we have suggested that for technical reasons the first dwellings cannot be completed for some time. The lag structure might therefore take the general form:

$$C_t^s = f(S_{t-3} \ldots S_{t-n})$$

or

$$C_t^s = f(S_{t-3} \ldots S_{t-n}, C_{t-1}).$$

It is also possible that suppliers attempt to overcome the technical difficulties of slow adjustment by anticipating changes in independent variables rather than waiting for the direct price evidence. Their ability to

119

change supply in anticipation will be determined by the normal factors which determine starts including financial constraints. Such a formulation does not exclude the possibility of lags in builders' reaction to changes in price and the determining variables but will result in apparently more rapid completions. All the structures discussed above were estimated. The results are now discussed.

8.1 Statistical estimation

We used the same methods of estimation for this equation as for the supply and demand equations. Firstly, ordinary least-squares estimates were made in order to provide a general picture of the relationships. Secondly the estimates were tested for autoregressive error and the relevant orders of autoregression were removed. Finally the most efficient estimates were used to determine the two-staged least-squares model to be used for analysis purposes.

Some ordinary least-squares estimates are presented in Table 8.2. Equation 1 was the simple Koyck transform specification assuming a minimum building time of six months. The adjustment process is very slow: only about 55 per cent of the units are completed within two years in addition to the 16 per cent included in the constant term. Equation 2 allows for the possibility of some dwellings being completed in less than six months either because builders anticipated changes in costs and prices, or because building can be more rapid. In this case although 22 per cent are completed within three months still only about 66 per cent (plus 14 per cent in the constant term) are finished at the end of two years. The estimated structure used in equation 3 is one possible version of the more general Jorgenson lag structure where the adjustment process is allowed to take any shape. The results again suggest 22 per cent of dwellings completed within the first quarter but only about seventyfive per cent of the starts in any one quarter are finished within two years. If further lags are added to the starts variable the sign on PS_{t-4} is negative and further lags are insignificant. The Durbin-Watson statistic and the large coefficient on PC_{t-1} in all versions suggest that the results may be very biased as a result of autocorrelation.

Equations 4 and 5 show different forms of a rational lag structure. In the first case where completions are constrained not to take place for six months PS_{t-3} to PS_{t-7} add to 75 per cent and over half of the completions are in the third quarter. The constant term accounts for a further 13,000 units, nearly 30 per cent of the average number of private comple-

Table 8.2

Completions/starts ordinary least-squares estimates

(59 observations, seasonal and first quarter 1963 dummies included in all equations)

1	$7053 \cdot 49$ (3·56)	$+ \; 0 \cdot 16 \, PS_{t-3}$ (2·21)	$+ \; 0 \cdot 75 \, C_{t-1}$ (8·84)	$+ \; Ds$				
			$\bar{r}^2 = 0 \cdot 93 \quad DW = 1 \cdot 45$					
2	$4015 \cdot 44$ (1·94)	$+ \; 0 \cdot 22 \, PS_{t-1}$ (2·98)	$+ \; 0 \cdot 68 \, PC_{t-1}$ (7·97)	$+ \; Ds$				
			$\bar{r}^2 = 0 \cdot 93 \quad DW = 2 \cdot 01$					
3	$6195 \cdot 87$ (3·33)	$+ \; 0 \cdot 22 \, PS_{t-1}$ (3·00)	$+ \; 0 \cdot 11 \, PS_{t-2}$ (1·51)	$+ \; 0 \cdot 14 \, PS_{t-3}$ (2·05)	$+ \; 0 \cdot 44 \, PC_{t-1}$ (3·98)	$+ \; Ds$		
			$\bar{r}^2 = 0 \cdot 95 \quad DW = 1 \cdot 58$					
4	$13018 \cdot 53$ (4·50)	$+ \; 0 \cdot 43 \, PS_{t-3}$ (4·36)	$+ \; 0 \cdot 15 \, PS_{t-4}$ (1·25)	$+ \; 0 \cdot 10 \, PS_{t-5}$ (0·81)	$+ \; 0 \cdot 07 \, PS_{t-6}$ (0·59)	$+ \; 0 \cdot 001 \, PS_{t-7}$ (0·01)	$+ \; Ds$	
			$\bar{r}^2 = 0 \cdot 85 \quad DW = 0 \cdot 68$					
5	$5246 \cdot 34$ (2·29)	$+ \; 0 \cdot 36 \, PS_{t-1}$ (5·48)	$+ \; 0 \cdot 15 \, PS_{t-2}$ (1·91)	$+ \; 0 \cdot 16 \, PS_{t-3}$ (2·04)	$+ \; 0 \cdot 04 \, PS_{t-4}$ (0·51)	$+ \; 0 \cdot 04 \, PS_{t-5}$ (0·44)	$+ \; 0 \cdot 07 \, PS_{t-6}$ (0·84)	$+ \; 0 \cdot 06 \, PS_{t-7}$ (0·96) $+ \; Ds$
			$\bar{r}^2 = 0 \cdot 94 \quad DW = 1 \cdot 20$					

121

tions per quarter. Thus the rational lag adds to more than 100 per cent on average, perhaps suggesting the existence of an omitted trend term. The Durbin-Watson statistic at 0·85 shows very high autocorrelation of the residuals giving further evidence of trend. Equation 5 has a similar structure but implies that the constraint on speed of building is relaxed. The constant term is reduced and on average a two-year period $(PS_t$ to $PS_{t-7})$ accounts for almost exactly 100 per cent of starts.

It is clear that all these results are inadequate and biased in that there is considerable autocorrelation but they still suggest that a finite rational lag has better explanatory power than the infinite lag structure which includes PC_{t-1} probably because such a term is really a misspecification of the existing first-order autocorrelation.

RALS was used to test for auto-correlation up to seventh-order. Only first-order autocorrelation was found to be significant. The chosen equations were then re-run on GIVE and the first-order autocorrelation bias removed.

The new results are presented in Table 8.3. The first three equations are versions of the infinite lag structure. Equations 1 and 2 are constrained to be the Koyck transform formulation. All have very large and significant constant terms accounting in 1 and 3 for three-quarters of average completions and in 2 for over 95 per cent. These together with the insignificance of all other variables, except the seasonal dummies, suggest that this type of lag structure is a complete misspecification of actuality and has little explanatory value. Indeed in, say, equation 1, roughly 10 per cent of all houses would still not be completed after ten years. These new estimates are most useful in showing the importance of determining and removing autocorrelation when a specification includes the lagged dependent variable. Indeed equation 2 is the only specification other than the Koyck transform versions where the lagged dependent variable has a positive sign. In all other versions PC_{t-1} is negative although not significantly different from zero (the coefficient was usually about 0·05). This suggests that there are few underlying difficulties resulting from the trend. More importantly there seems no case for continuing with this approach because of the large constant term and low significance of the independent variables. We thus accept that the earlier significance was simply the result of misspecification of the autoregressive error.

On the other hand equations 4 and 5 give very significant and stable results. PS_{t-7} is found to have a negative sign (equation 4) while being completely insignificant. Whatever lag structure was tested PS_{t-7} remained tiny and negative. We therefore assume that all private dwellings are completed by within eighteen to twenty-one months. The constant term (dwellings unassigned to a specific period) is now relatively small, although still significant. Excluding this 22 per cent of starts are completed within six months, a technically quite possible result but a higher percentage than expected from general discussions with experts in the industry. Although generally weights decline as the length of lag increases there is no simple exponential shape. This may reflect seasonal variations which have not been fully removed by the dummy adjustment, or there

Table 8.3

Completions/starts ordinary least-squares estimates with first-order autocorrelation removed

(56 observations, seasonal and first quarter 1963 dummies included in all equations)

1    $35422 \cdot 87$ + $0 \cdot 09 \, PS_{t-3}$ + $0 \cdot 14 \, PC_{t-1}$ + Ds
     $(4 \cdot 13)$ $(1 \cdot 56)$ $(1 \cdot 22)$

        $s = 2179 \cdot 52$ alpha $1 = 0 \cdot 93$
                    $(19 \cdot 61)$

2    $42694 \cdot 26$ + $0 \cdot 11 \, PS_{t-1}$ + $0 \cdot 002 \, PC_{t-1}$ + Ds
     $(5 \cdot 92)$ $(1 \cdot 33)$ $(0 \cdot 01)$

        $s = 2214 \cdot 18$ alpha $1 = 0 \cdot 92$
                    $(20 \cdot 13)$

3    $33441 \cdot 02$ + $0 \cdot 08 \, PS_{t-2}$ + $0 \cdot 10 \, PS_{t-3}$ + $0 \cdot 03 \, PS_{t-4}$ + $0 \cdot 14 \, PC_{t-1} + Ds$
     $(3 \cdot 56)$ $(1 \cdot 19)$ $(1 \cdot 63)$ $(0 \cdot 48)$ $(1 \cdot 11)$

        $s = 2192 \cdot 20$ alpha $1 = 0 \cdot 90$
                    $(13 \cdot 97)$

4    $9955 \cdot 12$ + $0 \cdot 22 \, PS_{t-1}$ + $0 \cdot 17 \, PS_{t-2}$ + $0 \cdot 18 \, PS_{t-3}$ + $0 \cdot 10 \, PS_{t-4}$
     $(5 \cdot 95)$ $(3 \cdot 04)$ $(2 \cdot 81)$ $(3 \cdot 04)$ $(1 \cdot 61)$

        + $0 \cdot 05 \, PS_{t-5}$ + $0 \cdot 09 \, PS_{t-6}$ − $0 \cdot 01 \, PS_{t-7} + Ds$
           $(0 \cdot 89)$ $(1 \cdot 63)$ $(0 \cdot 24)$

        $s = 2067 \cdot 90$ alpha $1 = 0 \cdot 59$
                    $(3 \cdot 67)$

5    $9796 \cdot 04$ + $0 \cdot 22 \, PS_{t-1}$ + $0 \cdot 17 \, PS_{t-2}$ + $0 \cdot 18 \, PS_{t-3}$ + $0 \cdot 09 \, PS_{t-4}$
     $(2 \cdot 22)$ $(3 \cdot 06)$ $(2 \cdot 85)$ $(3 \cdot 06)$ $(1 \cdot 61)$

        + $0 \cdot 05 \, PS_{t-5}$ + $0 \cdot 09 \, PS_{t-6}$ + Ds
           $(0 \cdot 88)$ $(1 \cdot 62)$

        $s = 2045 \cdot 53$ alpha $1 = 0 \cdot 59$
                    $(3 \cdot 64)$

could be technical reasons why once a unit is not finished within six months there is little need for hurry and so building takes longer. In equation 5, when the lag is limited to a maximum of twenty-one months, the constant term accounts for about 21 per cent of all completions and the coefficients on the lagged starts variable taken together add to 80 percent. In this formulation the lag structure adds to almost exactly 100 percent. The 's' value is only about 2,000 units suggesting a good estimation procedure. Finally very significant first-order autocorrelation has been removed. In all respects equation 5 appears to be a very adequate estimate of the process by which builders turn housing starts into the supply of completed dwellings for sale.

The ordinary least-squares estimates with autoregressive error removed suggest that only a rational lag structure is suitable for estimating the process of adjustment between starts and completions. The Koyck transform can be seen to be simply a misspecification of the autoregressive error, as are other specifications which include the lagged dependent variable. In the chosen rational lag structure all private dwellings are expected to be completed within twenty-one months while by far the greater proportion are completed within a year. The estimated lag structure suggests generally more rapid completion than do the first-in, first-out estimated lags found in the published data (Table 8.1). This is to be expected because the distribution around the mean is not normal. The estimated equation suggests that the speculative private builder builds a large percentage of dwellings fairly rapidly but may take quite a long time over a small proportion; possibly a profitable decision process.

After estimating many different formulations our final choice of equation to describe the lag between start and completion must be equation 5: a distributed six-period rational lag with first-order autocorrelation removed.

One possible modification of the simple rational lag so far analysed would be to include the financial dummies used in the other equations as surrogates for the general economic environment because this is said to affect the speed of construction. Many commentators have argued that when credit is difficult builders slow down final completions because purchasers cannot obtain a mortgage. If this were correct, we would expect to find that both MR and SR have negative signs and reduce completions by a significant amount. SR would be expected to reduce completions by a larger quantity than MR.

An offsetting effect might occur if builders are unable to start new work until funds for work-in-progress were released by sales. Then as finance gets more difficult to obtain builders would have to hurry comple-

124

tions in order to keep up their level of starts. However, as we have argued before, builders have less incentive than firms in most industries to keep an even level of work flowing and we would not therefore expect such an effect to be fully offsetting.

Table 8.4 shows the completions/starts equations with MR and SR included. Equation 1 uses the six-period rational lag structure; equation 2 the infinite lag formulation. Equation 1 is clearly the better formulation; C_{t-1} in equation 2 again being almost entirely insignificant. Both MR and SR have negative signs but both are insignificant at the 5 per cent level, although, as predicted, SR has more effect. Their inclusion reduces the 's' value in comparison with equation 5 in Table 8.3 by only 0·4 of 1 per cent — hardly a significant amount. The estimates suggest little reason for continuing with this hypothesis for even with strong rationing the effect is estimated at only about 4,750 per annum, roughly 2·5 per cent of total private completions.

When the flow of funds into building societies is included as a surrogate for builders' difficulty in selling the results are far more significant. The net flow of funds lagged two periods gives the most significant result decreasing the 's' value by over 6 per cent. The value of PS_{t-1} is increased from 22 per cent to 27 per cent suggesting that the houses that are normally finished most rapidly are most adversely affected by changes in financial stringency. The significance of the coefficients on all the first three lags is increased and the value of the constant term declines. The coefficients plus constant term add to about 99 per cent. In all ways this appears to be a suitable explanatory equation based on rational behaviour. It will therefore be included in further testing within the full model.

8.2 Conclusion

In this section we have looked at the specification of individual equations to explain the new private housing market. Each equation is based on economic analysis but there have had to be a number of simplifications and modifications to take account of problems of data and of testing. In the next section we attempt to bring these separate equations together into a full if simple model of the housing market. This can be used to help us examine the current situation, future trends and the effects of different government policies on new housing.

Table 8.4

The lag between starts and completions including financial variables

(56 observations, seasonal and first quarter 1963 dummies are included in all equations)

1 $9926 \cdot 95 + 0 \cdot 23\ PS_{t-1} + 0 \cdot 19\ PS_{t-2} + 0 \cdot 18\ PS_{t-3} + 0 \cdot 08\ PS_{t-4} + 0 \cdot 06\ PS_{t-5}$
   $(2 \cdot 86) \quad (3 \cdot 20) \qquad (3 \cdot 21) \qquad (3 \cdot 04) \qquad (1 \cdot 47) \qquad (0 \cdot 92)$
   $+ 0 \cdot 08\ PS_{t-6} - 693 \cdot 96\ MR - 1188 \cdot 95\ SR + Ds$
   $(1 \cdot 40) \qquad (0 \cdot 76) \qquad (1 \cdot 09)$
   alpha 1 = $0 \cdot 53$ $s = 2045 \cdot 13$
   $(3 \cdot 04)$

2 $9859 \cdot 02 + 0 \cdot 22\ PS_{t-1} + 0 \cdot 19\ PS_{t-2} + 0 \cdot 17\ PS_{t-3} + 0 \cdot 08\ PS_{t-4} + 0 \cdot 05\ PS_{t-5}$
   $(2 \cdot 90) \quad (2 \cdot 44) \qquad (3 \cdot 04) \qquad (2 \cdot 63) \qquad (1 \cdot 11) \qquad (0 \cdot 84)$
   $+ 0 \cdot 08\ PS_{t-6} + 0 \cdot 03\ PC_{t-1} + 745 \cdot 91\ MR - 1251 \cdot 31\ SR + Ds$
   $(1 \cdot 29) \qquad (0 \cdot 81) \qquad (1 \cdot 15) \qquad (1 \cdot 15)$
   alpha 1 = $0 \cdot 51$ $s = 2069 \cdot 12$
   $(2 \cdot 30)$

3 $9539 \cdot 89 + 0 \cdot 27\ PS_{t-1} + 0 \cdot 16\ PS_{t-2} + 0 \cdot 17\ PS_{t-3} + 0 \cdot 06\ PS_{t-4} + 0 \cdot 05\ PS_{t-5}$
   $(3 \cdot 93) \quad (3 \cdot 76) \qquad (2 \cdot 83) \qquad (2 \cdot 98) \qquad (1 \cdot 09) \qquad (0 \cdot 80)$
   $+ 0 \cdot 07\ PS_{t-6} + 14 \cdot 40\ FF_{t-2} + Ds$
   $(1 \cdot 26) \qquad (2 \cdot 41)$
   alpha 1 = $0 \cdot 40$ $s = 1939 \cdot 15$
   $(2 \cdot 04)$

Notes

[1] L.M. Koyck, *Distributed Lags and Investment Analysis*, North Holland Publishing Company, Amsterdam, 1954.

[2] See S. Almon, The Distributed Lag between Capital Appropriations and Expenditures; *Econometrica,* vol.33, no. 1 1965. For a general survey of the problems of distributed lags see Z. Griliches 'Distributed lags — A Survey', *Econometrica* vol. 35, no. 1, 1967.

[3] P. Schmidt, and R.N. Waud, 'The Almon Lag Technique and the Monetary versus Fiscal Policy Debate', *Journal of American Statistical Association*, vol.68, no.341, Applications section, 1973.

[4] See especially D.W. Jorgenson, 'Capital Theory and Investment Behaviour', *American Economic Review*, vol. L1X1, no.2, 1963.

[5] The method of collecting the data means that the completions variable is also affected by variation in start/completion time as a result of changes in demand because some builders do not completely finish a dwelling until it is actually sold. The house will thus not enter the statistics although fully constructed.

[6] See, e.g. M. Steuer, R.J. Ball, and J.R. Eaton, 'The Effect of Waiting Times in Foreign Orders for Machine Tools', *Economica*, vol. XXXIII, no. 132, 1966.

PART III

The Model and its Implications for Policy

9   The Two-Staged
Least-Squares Estimates

9.1   Introduction

In this section we examine the nature of the model in more detail. Until now we have been looking at each of the equations separately in order to determine the specification which gives the best empirical results on the basis of the underlying theoretical structure. We now attempt a more rigorous analysis of the results. This examination is divided into four parts.

Firstly the model is re-estimated using two-staged least squares. This removes the bias introduced by assuming variables endogenous to the full model can be treated as exogenous. It is then possible to assess adequately the importance of the estimated coefficients in determining demand and supply. Next we wish to discover whether the model is reasonably stable and is therefore a useful tool for forecasting purposes. This problem can be analysed either by estimating future years using the coefficients obtained from the model or by re-estimating the model using a longer data series and comparing the coefficients obtained. In this monograph the second method is used. Because the housing market has suffered so many structural changes in the past few years it is not expected that the coefficients will have remained stable. It should however be possible to analyse the changes that have taken place and assess whether these reflect such structural variations or whether they are more likely to be the result of inherent instability in the model.

Chapter 11 consists of an examination of the structural properties of the model to determine whether as defined it can simulate behaviour throughout the period of estimation; whether it can be employed for predictive purposes using simulation methods; and most important, whether it is possible to assess the effects of policy changes on the whole housing market by varying the values of particular independent variables.

Finally we will examine the nature of policy variations that have occurred during the last few years and some likely future changes. In the light of the models and other evidence we will assess the importance of these changes and the likely results both in the private sector and in the overall housing market.

9.2   Demand: problems and results

The nature of interdependence in the model derived from the demand and supply equations in the last section is not straightforward. In most of the earlier versions current price enters as part of the monthly repayment term *PM*. As current price is an explanatory variable in all versions of the supply of starts equation *P* must be treated as endogenous. But no programme can deal with *P* defined in different ways in each of the two equations. It is therefore necessary in the demand equation to separate *PM* into its component parts of price and the mortgage rate of interest. For this reason we have only estimated two-staged least-squares equations for the structural forms discussed in the final section of Chapter 6, 'Another possible demand structure'.

In these equations house prices often enter lagged by two quarters. Current price is still included however through the expectations term $DP\left[\dfrac{P_t - P_{t-1}}{P_t}\right]$. The model is therefore still simultaneously determined.

The completions-starts equation which relates supply of starts to the supply of completions has no current endogenous variables as regressors. As such the coefficients are unbiased and there is no requirement to re-estimate this section of the model.

The best two-staged least-squares demand results are given in Table 9.1. Equation 1 is strictly comparable with equation 1 in Table 6.7. The estimate of autoregressive error remains insignificant and almost exactly the same. The '*s*' value increases by 0·2 per cent, an almost totally insignificant amount. Thus the demand equation as a whole continues to have the same explanatory power. The only, very slight, differences are that the coefficient and significance of current price (as reflected in *DP*) increases while that of P_{t-2} declines.[1]

When the flow of funds is included (equation 2) the main difference is that in all cases the best estimate of the lag is now three-quarters rather than two as in some ordinary least-squares equations. Almost no other difference is discernible. No such change occurs when the Spencer and O'Herlihy dummies are substituted (equation 4). In this case again the only difference is that the value of *DP* increases slightly while that of P_{t-2} declines.

When population is introduced (equation 4) the only major difference is that the value of the constant term declines by 10,000 units. When both stock and population are included (equation 5) the reduction is less

Table 9.1 Two-staged least-squares estimates demand

1 $PC_t = 22230 \cdot 83 + 4 \cdot 12\,Y_t - 55 \cdot 37\,P_{t-2} - 1{,}357{,}351\,BSM_{t-2} + 64067 \cdot 34\,DP_t + 0 \cdot 70\,PC_{t-1}$
$\quad\quad\ \ (4 \cdot 50)\quad\ (2 \cdot 24)\quad\ (0 \cdot 79)\quad\quad (3 \cdot 54)\quad\quad\quad (2 \cdot 97)\quad\quad (9 \cdot 87)$
$\quad s = 2083 \cdot 10 \quad \text{alpha } 1 = 0 \cdot 16\ (1 \cdot 04)$

2 $PC_t = 22888 \cdot 76 + 3 \cdot 98\,Y_t - 71 \cdot 61\,P_{t-2} - 1{,}297{,}572\,BSM_{t-2} + 64199 \cdot 47\,DP + 0 \cdot 71\,PC_{t-1}$
$\quad\quad\ \ (4 \cdot 69)\quad\ (2 \cdot 21)\quad\ (1 \cdot 02)\quad\quad (3 \cdot 40)\quad\quad\quad (2 \cdot 94)\quad\quad (10 \cdot 20)$
$\quad\quad\quad\quad\quad\quad\quad\quad\quad\quad\quad + 9 \cdot 53\,FF_{t-3}$
$\quad\quad\quad\quad\quad\quad\quad\quad\quad\quad\quad\ \ (1 \cdot 14)$
$\quad s = 2076 \cdot 68 \quad \text{alpha} = 0 \cdot 14\ (0 \cdot 89)$

3 $PC_t = 20678 \cdot 79 + 2 \cdot 79\,Y_t - 28 \cdot 59\,P_{t-2} - 1{,}065{,}902\,BSM_{t-2} + 77{,}608 \cdot 60\,DP_t + 0 \cdot 74\,PC_{t-1}$
$\quad\quad\ \ (5 \cdot 31)\quad\ (1 \cdot 91)\quad\ (0 \cdot 53)\quad\quad (3 \cdot 41)\quad\quad\quad (3 \cdot 31)\quad\quad (13 \cdot 76)$
$\quad\quad\quad\ \ - 1345 \cdot 43\,MR \quad - 1803 \cdot 73\,MR \quad + 2398 \cdot 08\,SR$
$\quad\quad\quad\quad\quad\quad\quad\quad\quad (2 \cdot 84)\quad\quad (3 \cdot 68)$
$\quad s = 1898 \cdot 15 \quad \text{alpha } 1 = - 0 \cdot 09\ (0 \cdot 61)$

4 $PC = -85549 \cdot 37 + 1 \cdot 32\,Y_t - 54 \cdot 57\,P_{t-2} - 948{,}144\,BSM_{t-2} + 74{,}537 \cdot 93\,DP_t + 0 \cdot 67\,PC_{t-1}$
$\quad\quad\ \ (0 \cdot 92)\quad\ (0 \cdot 66)\quad\ (0 \cdot 92)\quad\quad (2 \cdot 83)\quad\quad\quad (1 \cdot 14)\quad\quad (8 \cdot 72)$
$\quad\quad - 1345 \cdot 43\,MR \quad - 1919 \cdot 70\,SR \quad + 2 \cdot 28\,N$
$\quad\quad\quad (1 \cdot 79)\quad\quad (2 \cdot 47)\quad\quad (1 \cdot 14)$
$\quad s = 1888 \cdot 33 \quad \text{alpha } 1 = - 0 \cdot 06\ (0 \cdot 36)$

5 $PC_t = -294351 \cdot 63 + 0 \cdot 27\,Y_t - 148 \cdot 48\,P_{t-2} - 55{,}738 \cdot 8\,BSM_{t-2} + 60562 \cdot 37\,DP_t + 0 \cdot 55\,PC_{t-1}$
$\quad\quad\ \ (3 \cdot 23)\quad\ (0 \cdot 11)\quad\ (2 \cdot 28)\quad\quad (1 \cdot 35)\quad\quad\quad (3 \cdot 01)\quad\quad (6 \cdot 80)$
$\quad\quad + 17 \cdot 93\,FF_{t-3} \quad + 7 \cdot 87\,N_t \quad - 3 \cdot 78\,ST_{t-1}$
$\quad\quad\quad (2 \cdot 31)\quad\quad (2 \cdot 89)\quad\quad (0 \cdot 77)$
$\quad s = 1863 \cdot 96 \quad \text{alpha } 1 = 0 \cdot 09\ (0 \cdot 53)$

133

marked. Otherwise the values and significance of the independent coefficients remain very stable.

One conclusion that can be drawn from these results is that the bias introduced by using ordinary least-squares estimates is very small indeed. We can therefore accept without much reservation the results obtained in the earlier estimates where monthly repayments are used as the independent variable instead of price and the mortgage rate separately. On the basis of this indirect evidence we can now put more faith in the conclusions reached in Chapter 6.

Having obtained unbiased estimates of the coefficients we can now examine the responsiveness of new private completions to changes is each of the independent variables. Table 9.2. shows the values of the elasticities of completions to each of the relevant independent variables. The values vary quite considerably, especially in the case of income when population and stock are included. This reflects the trend term aspect of the variable. None of the estimates suggest that income elasticity relating to the demand for new housing is anything like as high as unity. But in assessing the importance of this result we should remember that the estimates relate to the number of new dwellings rather than increased expenditure.[2]

The price elasticity is also quite small and is generally dwarfed by the effect of the mortgage rate. These very high elasticities ranging from two up to five suggest that the interest rate is dominant in determining demand. The value declines when availability variables are added but in all versions it remains at least eight times as important as any other variable. The elasticity on the flow of funds on the other hand is never more than 0·1.[3]

A 1 per cent increase in the rate of change of house prices leads to about a 0·3 per cent increase in the demand for new completions, a relatively large reaction in comparison with say the effect of changes in the level

Table 9.2

Demand elasticities (dependent variable PC_t)

Equation (no. from Table 9.1)	Income	Price	Mortgage rate	Rate of change of prices
1	0·56	− 0·22	− 5·02	0·31
2	0·53	− 0·29	− 4·80	0·31
3	0·38	− 0·15	− 3·94	0·37
4	0·20	− 0·22	− 3·51	0·36
5	0·01	− 0·59	− 2·06	0·29

of house prices although still small in comparison with the effect of the mortgage rate. The value of the elasticity on the expectations variable is relatively constant as is its significance measured by the 't' statistic. The significance of the other variables is less stable and this is reflected in the variability of the values of the elasticities. In general we claim no more for these results than that they probably reflect the relative importance of the independent variables correctly. It will now be interesting to assess whether the specification is stable over time.

Before looking at the effect of adding 1971 and 1972 we digress to examine whether using real rather than money values as determining variables is more satisfactory. In general the results do not show any great differences. An example is given in Table 9.3. The effect of price is even less significant than in the equations in money terms (and indeed in many versions the sign is no longer negative). The most important factor is that the effect of the mortgage rate is greatly reduced suggesting perhaps that its specification should also be changed to take account of the difference between real and money rates. The significance of the variables and the overall standard error does not suggest that this specification is obviously better than that which we have concentrated upon up to now. We will examine the value of this specification in more detail when looking at the results to 1972.

9.3 Supply

In the supply equation there are no problems in estimating the two-staged least-squares values. All the equations include current house prices and no other endogenous variables are used. The estimation procedure is therefore very straightforward.

Table 9.3

Demand — deflated price (an example)

$$PC_t = -151685 + 1118 \cdot 25\, YR_t - 6515\, PR_{t-2} - 558000\, BSM_{t-2} + 41362\, DP$$
$$(1 \cdot 27) \quad (2 \cdot 45) \quad\quad (0 \cdot 65) \quad\quad (0 \cdot 99) \quad\quad (2 \cdot 16)$$

$$+ 22 \cdot 00\, FF_{t-3} - 13 \cdot 74\, ST_{t-1} + 6 \cdot 94\, N_t + 0 \cdot 80\, PC_{t-1}$$
$$(2 \cdot 80) \quad\quad (3 \cdot 73) \quad\quad (1 \cdot 99) \quad\quad (4 \cdot 25)$$

$$\text{alpha } 1 = 0 \cdot 30 \quad s = 1769$$
$$(1 \cdot 55)$$

Table 9.4

Two-staged least-squares estimates — Supply

1	$PS_t = 65781 \cdot 14$ $(3 \cdot 92)$	$-\ 5166 \cdot 80\, r_{t-1}$ $(2 \cdot 66)$	$+\ 567 \cdot 04\, P_t$ $(2 \cdot 76)$	$-\ 515 \cdot 71\, CC_t$ $(1 \cdot 97)$
		$s = 3698 \cdot 98$	alpha $1 = 0 \cdot 86$ $(12 \cdot 96)$	
2	$PS_t = 67583 \cdot 58$ $(4 \cdot 01)$	$-\ 4536 \cdot 75\, r_{t-1}$ $(2 \cdot 32)$	$-\ 570 \cdot 61\, CC_t$ $(2 \cdot 16)$	$+\ 588 \cdot 21\, P_t$ $(2 \cdot 87)$
			$-\ 1371 \cdot 90\, MR_t$ $(0 \cdot 95)$	$-\ 2988 \cdot 04\, SR_t$ $(1 \cdot 55)$
		$s = 3676 \cdot 53$	alpha $1 = 0 \cdot 86$ $(12 \cdot 64)$	
3	$PS_t = 74890 \cdot 89$ $(4 \cdot 03)$	$-\ 4363 \cdot 38\, r_{t-1}$ $(2 \cdot 26)$	$+\ 419 \cdot 79\, P_t$ $(1 \cdot 56)$	$-\ 493 \cdot 01\, CC_t$ $(1 \cdot 58)$
				$+\ \ \ 38 \cdot 11\, FF_{t-2}$ $(2 \cdot 70)$
		$s = 3521 \cdot 07$	alpha $1 = 0 \cdot 87$ $(13 \cdot 16)$	

The most important results are shown in Table 9.4. There are only tiny changes in the values of the coefficients and in the standard error of the estimate. The importance of the cost of credit increases very slightly as does that of construction costs while the coefficient on P_t declines by a small amount. When the availability variables are included all other coefficients decline slightly as does the value of the constant term. The results suggest there was little bias in the original estimates and conclusions drawn about other specifications can be regarded as upheld.

When we examine the calculated elasticities in Table 9.5 the results are roughly what might be expected. The response to a 1 per cent change in the cost of funds (r_{t-1}) is less than unity and is smaller than that expected from changes in either prices or construction costs. But of course large changes in the rate of interest are more likely.

In the supply equations the value of the elasticities are far more stable than in the demand equations — mainly because the specifications tested are not very different from one another. Once again we must remember that the values should be treated with care even though almost all the coefficients are significant at the 5 per cent level. The only exceptions are in equation 3 where the values of both price and construction costs decline.

136

Table 9.5

Supply elasticities (dependent variable PS_t)

Equation (from Table 9.3)	r_{t-1}	P_t	CC_t
1	− 0·72	1·93	− 1·65
2	− 0·64	1·94	− 1·88
3	− 0·61	1·43	− 1·56

Although the flow of funds variable has a significant coefficient its importance is very limited, the measured elasticity in equation 3 is only 0·12. But again large changes in the independent variable might be expected.

The importance of these stable, significant coefficients is great but there is a real continuing problem in the large and significant constant term which suggests that we have not been able to discover all the relevant determining variables. Overall there are very few changes as a result of removing ordinary least-squares bias but this is not surprising because the interaction of current endogenous variables is very small.

The alternative version of the supply equation to bring it in line with the demand equation in real terms requires that we substitute PR for P and CR for C. As with the demand equation there is very little change in the overall significance of the equation. But there are more changes in the values of coefficients on the supply side and these are generally for the better. Examples are given in Table 9.6. The most important factor is that

Table 9.6

Supply − deflated price

1 $PS = 20{,}244\cdot41 \quad - \quad 4782\cdot23\, r_{t-1} \quad + \quad 64952\cdot48\, PR_t \quad - \quad 22944\cdot60\, CR_t$
   $(0\cdot56) \qquad\qquad\qquad (2\cdot90) \qquad\qquad\qquad (2\cdot95) \qquad\qquad\qquad (0\cdot60)$

   alpha 1 = 0·82 $s = 3680\cdot40$
   $(10\cdot67)$

2 $PS = 52{,}182\cdot86 \quad - \quad 5104\cdot30\, r_{t-1} \quad + \quad 60{,}031\cdot26\, PR_t \quad - \quad 46{,}041\cdot60\, CR_t$
   $(1\cdot35) \qquad\qquad\qquad (3\cdot17) \qquad\qquad\qquad (2\cdot70) \qquad\qquad\qquad (1\cdot20)$

   $+ \quad 33\cdot31\, FF_{t-2}$
   $(2\cdot37)$

   alpha 1 = 0·84 $s = 3525\cdot95$
   $(12\cdot02)$

the value of the constant term is reduced dramatically without changing the standard error of the estimate. The importance of the rate of interest increases while that of construction costs declines. The elasticities are still about the same being -0.67 and -0.71 for r_{t-1}, 0.75 and 1.62 for PR_t and 0.6 and 1.56 for CR_t. These results suggest that we should not forget about analysing the model in real value terms, even though the results are not impressive on the demand side. We will examine this specification again when we look at 1971 and 1972, which we now do.

Notes

[1] The relationship between DP and P_{t-2} is complicated by the fact that when determining DP, P_{t-1} is constrained to be negative. This constraint should affect the value of the coefficient on P_{t-2}. Modifying the estimation procedure so that P_t is treated as endogenous is therefore expected to have some offsetting effect on the value of P_{t-2}, as it does.

[2] These conclusions are roughly in line with the estimates for the UK obtained by Byatt and others at the Department of the Environment. Their estimates however were on a cross-section sample and one would expect them to be lower in comparison with time-series results. See I.C.R. Byatt, A. E. Holmans and D. Laidler 'Income and the Demand for Housing: Some Evidence for Great Britain' in M. Parkin (ed.) Association of University Teachers in Economics Conference Aberystwyth 1972, *Essays in Modern Economics*, Longmans, London 1973.

[3] This does not make the flow of funds unimportant however as it is quite normal for this variable to change by very large amounts.

10 · The Years 1971 and 1972

10.1 Introduction

In this chapter we look at the effects on the model of adding an extra two years' observations, those of 1971 and 1972. If no structural changes had taken place during those two years and the model were an accurate reflection of the private new housing market the coefficients would remain much the same, although we would still expect some minor variations as a result of random changes in the independent variables. If the coefficients do not remain reasonably stable we have two possible hypotheses: that the model is an inadequate reflection of the new private housing market or that structural changes have taken place in the market which affect the original specification. In this case the model may still be a perfectly reasonable explanation of the housing market between 1955 and 1970 and will still give useful indications of the nature of the effects of likely changes in independent variables. It will however be of little use for forecasting purposes. What will be necessary then will be an analysis of the structural changes that have taken place and an attempt to assess how and why these changes have affected the behaviour of the private new housing market.

The years 1971 and 1972 are particularly difficult years against which to test our model because very large and rapid changes did take place in certain of the more important independent variables. In particular house prices started to rise very rapidly in 1971 and by the end of 1972 they were 65 per cent higher than at the end of 1970 (while in the five years before they had only risen 25 per cent overall).[1] At the same time the general price level also rose rapidly although nothing like as fast as in the housing sector. This inflationary pressure, which was expected to continue, meant that the benefit of buying an asset, especially one which appeared to be increasing in value faster than the general price level as did housing, was very great. There was thus considerable pressure on the market caused by people trying to buy second homes, by owner-occupiers wishing to move up in the market, and by first-time purchasers who saw the gains from owner-occupation increasing. At the same time savings expanded partly as a consequence of rapidly increasing money incomes and partly apparently as a result of precautionary behaviour in the face of inflationary pressure. The net flow of funds to building societies thus went up very fast and it was not until late 1972 that savers began to realise that the real rate of interest was falling and to shift their money into other financial assets. Pressure on mortgage rates thus did not commence until the very end of the period under discussion. These large changes in the value of certain independent variables and constancy of others caused by lags in building societies' and savers' reactions mean that the 1971 and 1972 observations are likely to be way off the estimated regression line whatever the structure of the underlying model. For this reason it would have been very much more use in testing the general adequacy of the model if the additional years' observations had not been so abnormal. Such large variations may well mean that when looking back in future years 1971 and 1972 will have to be regarded as a special case rather than a true reflection of the underlying behaviour of the new housing market.

There were also a number of structural changes in the existing housing situation. The two most important, discussed in section one, were the introduction of the Housing Finance Act which changed the nature of subsidies to the public sector and to tenants in general, and the increased emphasis on improvement subsidies in both the public and private sectors. The effect of the Housing Finance Act (and the earlier expectation of its becoming law) was to increase the cost of remaining in rental accommodation for higher income public and private tenants. They therefore had an extra incentive to shift into owner-occupation. The effect of improvement grants was to put pressure on certain types of labour particularly plumbing and electrical skills. As repairs and maintenance became relatively profitable building workers moved into this sector and away from actual building. Partially as a result of this the speed of new building declined and extra pressure was put on the new housing market. We expect these facts to be reflected in changes in the coefficients of independent variables in all equations.

10.2 Demand

Table 10.1 shows various estimates of the demand equation in money terms once 1971 and 1972 are included. Although in general the standard error of the estimate only increases slightly (by about 2·5 per cent) the structural form changes rather considerably, and not for the better in terms of explanatory power.

Equation 2 is strictly comparable with equation 1 in Table 9.1. There

140

Table 10.1

Demand in Money Terms 1955–72 (dependent variable PC_t, 67 observations)

1 38,846·67 + 2·91 Y_t − 40·28 P_t + 1285·46 DP_t − 42498·25 BSM_t + 0·18 PC_{t-1} + Ds
   (3·18)   (1·70)   (0·94)   (1·11)   (0·92)   (1·57)

   alpha 1 = 0·91 $s = 2152·56$
            (16·46)

2 36,093·18 + 4·44 Y_t − 139·08 P_{t-2} − 125252·73 BS_{t-2} + 17482·12 DP + 0·21 PC_{t-1} + Ds
   (2·97)   (2·50)   (2·01)   (0·27)   (1·63)   (1·93)

   alpha 1 = 0·91 $s = 2151·19$
            (17·25)

3 36,381·87 + 4·31 Y_t − 136·11 P_{t-2} − 110170·1 BS_{t-2} + 15264·44 DP_t + 0·64 FF_{t-3} + Ds
   (2·92)   (2·33)   (1·96)   (0·23)   (1·29)   (0·08)
                                                                        + 0·22 PC_{t-1}
                                                                          (1·84)

   alpha 1 = 0·91 $s = 2163·36$
            (17·26)

4 213,193·00 + 2·73, Y_t − 149·43 P_{t-2} − 916656·22 BS_{t-2} + 18·68 FF_{t-3} + 26820·95 DP + Ds
   (2·95)   (2·23)   (3·95)   (2·47)   (2·27)   (1·04)
               + 6·15 N_t − 4·10 ST_{t-1} + 0·65 PC_{t-1}
                 (2·42)   (0·98)   (8·58)

   alpha 1 = − 0·12 $s = 2062·35$
            (0·69)

are three important changes to be analysed. Firstly the importance of price increases varies considerably. This is to be expected in a time of rapidly changing house prices and suggests that in the last couple of years price rather than costs and availability of credit has become the dominant rationing factor. It is interesting to note however that the most significant formulation is still P_{t-2}. When P_t is used instead (equation 1) the value attached to the coefficient is reduced very considerably. This lag presumably continues to reflect the decision and transaction time lag implicit in the purchase of an asset which is so costly in comparison with most people's income. The second important difference is in the significance of the mortgage rate. The coefficient which had been extremely significant until 1970 becomes not significantly different from zero at the 5 per cent level once 1971 and 1972 are included. This may well reflect a lagged reaction in building society behaviour rather than an actual change in the underlying significance of the mortgage rate. In the period 1970 − 72 the rate hardly changed at all (in fact it actually went down 0·5 per cent for six months later in the period). Yet interest rates generally were rising and the rate of inflation was increasing also. Because hardly any change in rate was observed the coefficient cannot be expected to pick up the response which has in fact been transferred to the constant term (where the absolute value and significance have both increased). This result suggests that the effect of mortgage rate changes is being undervalued because of the lagged response of building societies. Before accepting that interest rates are not an important determinant of demand one would like to re-estimate the model including the period when the societies did react − 1973 and 1974. Until this is possible one cannot say whether 1955 − 70 or 1955 − 72 is a better estimate but because of the lack of change in 1971 and 1972 one would be inclined to use the former for estimation and forecasting purposes until further evidence is forthcoming.[2] The third difference is in the significance of the inflation variable itself. As the rate of change of house prices increases, the importance of the speculative effect appears to decline − perhaps because the rise in the level of house prices has seemed too rapid to many purchasers. The asset thus begins to appear relatively overpriced and in the end we might even expect the sign to change.

Similar results are to be found in equation 3 which corresponds with equation 2 of Table 9.1. The flow of funds reflecting availability of credit has also become insignificant perhaps because there was such an inflow over the period that it can hardly be seen as a constraint. If *MR* and *SR* are included instead of the flow of funds they are found to be completely insignificant and in the case of *SR* have the wrong sign. This suggests that the ex-post surrogate cannot reflect even as well as the flow of funds variable the administrative complexities and lags in reaction of building society behaviour.

Equation 4 (which is equivalent to equation 5 in Table 9.1) is by far the best explanation of demand. All the variables except the rate of change of prices and existing stock are significant and have the expected sign. The apparent adequacy of the formulation and the comparability with the earlier equation suggests that the trend variables are of great importance and that perhaps their inclusion allows better specification of the other variables.[3] The estimated equation suggests that the major structural change has occurred in reaction to the rate of change of prices. This is in line with the theoretical predictions in Chapter 4 which suggested that consumers might well change from being speculators to being risk averters as the rate of change of house prices increased.

The elasticities given in Table 10.2 bring further into focus the changes that we have discussed. Income continues to have very much the same effect on demand while price becomes far more important. All other variables (except population and existing stock where they remain stable) show very much lower elasticities. In the case of the mortgage rate we reserve judgement as to whether lagged reaction means that 1971 and 1972 are extraordinarily atypical. But in the case of the rate of change of prices we argue that what has been found is a structural change in behaviour as a result of very rapid changes in the rate of inflation.

Table 10.3 shows the equivalent equations when incomes and house prices are deflated by the retail price index. The equations estimated are comparable to those of Table 9.3. The importance of income is somewhat increased and the elasticities (shown in Table 10.4) are very close to unity. Deflated disposable income reflects real purchasing power and can be regarded as a better estimation of the responsiveness of demand to income than the monetary formulations assessed up to now. Once house prices

Table 10.2

Elasticities of demand 1955−72

Equation (no. from Table 10.1)	Income	Price $(t-2)$	Mortgage rate	Rate of change of price	Flow of funds
1	0·39	− 0·15 (P_t)	− 0·01	−	−
2	0·60	− 0·60	− 0·04	0·007	−
3	0·58	− 0·49	− 0·04	0·006	0·002
4	0·37	− 0·54	− 0·27	0·01	0·07

Table 10.3
Demand 1955−72 (deflated price)
(dependent variable PC_t − 67 observations)

1 $1923\cdot63 + 1013\cdot35\,YR_t - 6572\cdot92\,PR_t + 4397\cdot03\,DPR_t - 143{,}704\cdot98\,BSM_t + 0\cdot65\,PC_{t-1} + Ds$
  $(0\cdot78)\quad(4\cdot82)\qquad(1\cdot46)\qquad(1\cdot13)\qquad(3\cdot52)\qquad(7\cdot71)$
  $\text{alpha } 1 = -0\cdot17\qquad s = 2223\cdot68$
  $\qquad\qquad\;(0\cdot92)$

2 $16895\cdot74 + 869\cdot24\,YR_t - 13937\cdot19\,PR_{t-2} + 2561\cdot69\,DPR_t - 25862\cdot43\,BSM_{t-2} + 0\cdot24\,PC_{t-1} + Ds$
  $(1\cdot28)\quad(3\cdot34)\qquad(1\cdot44)\qquad(2\cdot31)\qquad(0\cdot59)\qquad(2\cdot15)$
  $\text{alpha } 1 = 0\cdot88\qquad s = 2095\cdot08$
  $\qquad\qquad(12\cdot17)$

3 $7830\cdot69 + 722\cdot00\,YR_t - 3731\cdot43\,PR_{t-2} + 5471\cdot11\,DPR_t - 114222\cdot72\,BSM_{t-3} + 10\cdot69\,FF_{t-3} + Ds$
  $(2\cdot05)\quad(3\cdot54)\qquad(0\cdot54)\qquad(2\cdot36)\qquad(4\cdot29)\qquad(1\cdot58)$
  $\qquad\qquad\qquad\qquad\qquad\qquad + 0\cdot60\,PC_{t-1}$
  $\qquad\qquad\qquad\qquad\qquad\qquad\;\;(8\cdot06)$
  $\text{alpha } 1 = 0\cdot09\qquad s = 1815\cdot77$
  $\qquad\qquad(0\cdot55)$

4 $348991\cdot32 + 878\cdot59\,YR_t - 11826\cdot89\,PR_{t-2} + 1741\cdot51\,DPR_t - 14016\cdot48\,BS_{t-2} + 4\cdot19\,FF_{t-3} + Ds$
  $(2\cdot64)\quad(3\cdot08)\qquad(1\cdot40)\qquad(1\cdot49)\qquad(0\cdot29)\qquad(0\cdot55)$
  $+ 11\cdot75\,N_t - 15\cdot22\,ST_{t-1} + 0\cdot38\,PC_{t-1}$
  $\;(2\cdot63)\qquad(2\cdot32)\qquad(2\cdot43)$
  $\text{alpha } 1 = 0\cdot51\qquad s = 1931\cdot65$
  $\qquad\qquad(2\cdot45)$

Table 10.4

Elasticities of demand 1955—72 (deflated prices)

Equation (no. from Table 10.3)	YR	PR	BSM
1	1·01	− 0·20	− 0·04
2	0·87	− 0·42	− 0·01
3	0·72	− 0·11	− 0·03
4	0·88	− 0·35	− 0·01

are deflated by the retail price index their effect is not significant at the 5 per cent level although the coefficient is certainly increased in importance by adding 1971 and 1972. Perhaps the difference between the effect in the deflated and monetary equations can be explained by the interrelationship between price and income, for the mortgage rules mean that income constraints may well have exactly the same effect on demand as price increases. The relative importance of the rate of change of prices is still shown to have declined although it is generally significant at the 10 per cent level (unlike in the monetary value based equations). The importance of the mortgage rate varies greatly depending on the specification and suggests only that the current formulation is unsatisfactory for forecasting purposes for the reasons already discussed.

In general the deflated price demand equations have marginally better explanatory power than the monetary equations but the difference is not significant.

Our main conclusion on the basis of the re-estimated demand equations is that the model is not adequately stable to be used for forecasting without further analysis. This should concentrate particularly on the cost and availability of credit where many structural changes have been taking place. These mean that it is hardly surprising that the results are not stable as we can only expect stable results in relatively constant structural conditions. We will examine the implications of these results further in the final chapter.

10.3 Completions − starts

The re-estimation of the completions-starts equation when 1971 and 1972

Table 10.5

Completions − starts 1955−72 (dependent variable PC_t − 65 observations)

1	15496·53	+ 0·18 S_{t-1}	+ 0·14 S_{t-2}	+ 0·16 S_{t-3}	+ 0·07 S_{t-4}
	(2·33)	(2·66)	(2·27)	(2·75)	(1·25)
			+ 0·06 S_{t-5}	+ 0·08 S_{t-6}	+ Ds
			(1·09)	(1·33)	
		alpha 1 = 0·78 s = 2089·45			
		(5·98)			
2	19076·61	+ 0·16 S_{t-1}	+ 0·11 S_{t-2}	+ 0·13 S_{t-3}	+ 0·05 S_{t-4}
	(2·30)	(2·47)	(1·73)	(2·19)	(0·81)
		+ 0·05 S_{t-5}	+ 0·08 S_{t-6}	+ 5·92 FF_{t-2}	+ Ds
		(0·94)	(1·31)	(1·09)	
		alpha 1 = 0·78 s = 2089·45			
		(5·98)			

are included can be found in Table 10.5. Equation 1 is comparable with equation 5 in Table 8.3. The overall explanatory power of the equation has declined very slightly (by less than 2 per cent). The main differences lie in the increased value of the constant term and decline in value of the coefficient in PS_{t-1}. This suggests that the general belief that building time has increased is perhaps incorrect and that what has actually happened is that more are built within three months (included in the constant term) and the rest are built more slowly. This would perhaps be expected in the bouyant selling market of 1971 and 1972 but suggests that the labour constraint affects numbers of starts rather than building times. Equation 2 is comparable with equation 3 in Table 8.4. Again the results are reasonably stable except for PS_{t-1} and the constant term. There is slight confirmatory evidence that if not built quickly houses take longer to build than they used to. But perhaps the most important deduction from equation 2 is that the importance of the flow of funds has declined. This again reflects the fact that funds were extraordinarily easy to obtain in the period 1971 − 72 and before we are prepared to accept its insignificance we would wish to examine builders' reactions in 1973 and 1974. Until that is possible one perhaps would accept the evidence of the 1955 − 70 estimates more readily.

10.4 Supply

The re-estimated supply equation can be found in Table 10.6. This is perhaps the most worrying set of results and reflects the poverty of the data base for supply estimation. Equation 1 is comparable with equation 1 in Table 9.4, and equation 2 with equation 3 in Table 9.4. The standard error of the estimate has increased by well over 10 per cent and the significance of all the variables has declined. The most important factor is the enormous decline in the importance of construction costs. This suggests that the index is no longer a viable reflection of costs because of the increasing importance of land prices (which went up by over 100 per cent in the period $1971 - 72$). As a result land probably drowned the effect of all other cost variables especially as there was little credit constraint and the rate of interest was relatively low in comparison with the actual rate of

Table 10.6

Supply of starts 1955–72 (dependent variable PS_t – 67 observations)

1	51892·59	–	2976·86 r_{t-1}	+	144·50 P_t	–	73·92 CC_t
	(3·72)		(1·57)		(1·78)		(0·46)
						+	Ds

alpha 1 = 0·85 $s = 4277·34$
(12·94)

2	49645·42	–	2925·92 r_{t-1}	+	119·06 P_t	–	45·32 CC_t
	(3·64)		(1·54)		(1·44)		(0·29)
				+	10·57 FF_{t-2}	+	Ds
					(0·96)		

alpha 1 = 0·84 $s = 4272·88$
(12·74)

Table 10.7

Elasticities of supply 1955–72

Equation (no. from Table 10.6)	r	P	CC
1	– 0·42	0·51	– 0·24
2	– 0·41	0·42	– 0·15

inflation. Table 10.7 shows the elasticities which reflect the poor quality of the estimation.

Tables 10.8 and 10.9 show the results when deflated price rather than monetary house prices are included. The results are comparable with Table 9.6 and are rather better than in the monetary based equations. Construction costs remain insignificant but house prices which reflect real profitability are significant and have an elasticity of close to unity. The effect of the rate of interest is unchanged. This certainly appears a better specification on the supply side but no starts equation is going to be truly satisfactory until adequate information on construction costs including land is obtainable.

Overall there have been rather large changes observed in both the demand and the supply equations. We therefore cannot use either model for forecasting purposes without further analysis. This takes two forms: analysing the internal stability of the model through simulation tests and examining the structural changes that have taken place in the last few years to assess their effect on the model and to determine how a more

Table 10.8

Supply of starts 1955−72 (deflated price) (dependent variable PS_t − 67 observations)

1	25,490·19	− 2693·31 r_{t-1}	+ 32972·74 PR_t	− 41·18 CC_t		
	(2·11)	(1·45)	(2·34)	(0·34)		
		alpha 1 = 0·82	$s = 4195·41$			
		(11·03)				
2	27,276·04	− 2684·59 r_{t-1}	+ 30715·75 PR_t	− 46·99 CC_t	+ 12·25 FF_{t-2}	
	(2·38)	(1·45)	(2·22)	(0·39)	(1·15)	
		alpha 1 = 0·81	$s = 4179·68$			
		(11·03)				

Table 10.9

Elasticities of supply 1955−72 (deflated price)

Equation (no. from Table 10.8)	r	P	CC
1	− 0·38	0·99	− 0·15
2	− 0·38	0·92	− 0·15

148

accurate reflection of reality might be obtained. We turn to these possibilities now.

Notes

[1] This 65 per cent increase masks a very wide variation between regions. For instance it was said that in the south east region including London house prices rose by at least 100 per cent.

[2] Another possibility would be to use a more general short-term interest rate to reflect expectations of changes in the mortgage rate. This would only be a surrogate and would not reflect the special institutional circumstances.

[3] The population data has been modified in these equations to take account of the new estimates of population since 1963 provided by the Registrar General in the light of the 1971 Census returns.

11 The Model as an Instrument for Analysing Policy

11.1 Introduction

Simulation methods can be helpful for three purposes. First, they can be used to test the overall stability of the model. This is done by providing the lagged values of endogenous variables, the coefficients and the actual values of exogenous variables over the original period of estimation. The values of the endogenous variables over this period are then estimated and compared with the actual observations. The closer the fit the greater the overall consistency and stability of the model. This type of testing is useful as the 't' statistics, r^2 s and 's' values calculated for individual coefficients and single equations are only partial indicators, even when two-staged least-squares are calculated. The simulation errors allow us to evaluate the model in the same way as residual errors of estimation for individual equations.[1]

Secondly, we can examine the effect on the endogenous variables over time of changes in the values of particular exogenous variables. This is done by simulating the estimated model for a number of periods. Changes can then be made in the input data for given variables and the results compared with the original model. These changes can be of two types, those which reflect possible policy variations and those which, without necessarily being controllable, show up more clearly the working of the system.

Thirdly, values of the endogenous variables outside the original period of observation can be obtained if those for the exogenous variables are either already known or can be predicted. The model can then be used for short-term forecasting. We will not however discuss this aspect of simulation further as we have already examined the limitations of the model for forecasting purposes in the current form in Chapter 10.

The method used in this chapter is derived from the simulation techniques first employed in the macro-economic models of Adelman and Adelman and Duesenberry, Eckstein and Fromm.[2] Both introduced random shocks to the system but the second concentrated on showing the effect of changes in policy variables. In a later work Fromm and Taubman[3] discussed simulation experiments made on the Brookings Institute model of the US economy. In the residential construction sector tests were limited to tracing the effect of the financial variables and their relative importance to demand and supply. They also pointed out that it is necessary to integrate the housing and financial sectors which were shown to be closely interdependent. Lawrence Smith has attempted to do this in his model of the Canadian housing and mortgage markets.[4] His work suggests that it might be possible to extend the model estimated here simply by adding equations determining the cost and availability of credit on both the supply and demand sides rather than by building a full-scale financial sector model.

Huang and McCarthy[5] have also tried partial analysis of the housing market using simulation methods to assess the effects of changes in financial variables in the home loan market in the USA.

The FBR-MIT model[6] looked at the problem in a much more general context. It was mainly interested in assessing the overall effects of monetary policy measures. The difference between their model and others lies in distinguishing between the service of housing and its investment qualities. Even though they built a full financial sector model they felt that a more elaborate treatment of financial intermediaries and housing credit was necessary before useful results could be obtained.

M. Desai[7] used simulation methods on a particular commodity market, tin, and showed the effect of certain possible policies. The use of simulation in this analysis closely follows Desai's work. It applies only to a single market and it is not possible to discuss its relationship to other markets except through assumed exogenous variable changes. Thus published simulation work falls into two groups: those where the authors wish to test the internal coherence of the model and those where the stress is laid on comparing simulated models in which particular exogenous variables have been varied. Within this group there are again two types: those like the FBR-MIT model which analyse the effect of economy-wide policy changes and those that concentrate on assessing the effect on particular markets of policies specific to those markets. All of these types of analyses are possible in relation to models of the form discussed in this monograph.

The model includes three types of independent variable (a) lagged endogenous variables, (b) exogenous variables which are not directly affected by government policies specific to the housing market and (c) policy variables. In determining the ability of the government to modify the behaviour of the housing market in the short-run it is only the third type that are relevant. Variables such as income and population which

152

come under (b) are of interest in medium-term forecasting but are un-likely to cause large changes in the housing sector in the immediate future: they can be treated as trend variables. The three most important factors to some extent within the government's control are: interest rates both for mortgages and builders, stock (via the public sector's building programme) and land prices. The second is directly under local authority control but is much affected by central government monetary and taxa-tion/subsidy policies. The third has not yet been employed as a central government policy variable but is likely to be used in the next few years. Changes in rates of interest have normally been brought about for pur-poses related to overall economic stability rather than directed specifica-lly at the housing market. But as its effect on housing has become more obvious in the last few years there has been a movement towards acting directly on, at least, the mortgage interest rates. For this reason and because of the importance of the cost of credit as shown in the model we concentrate in this chapter on the effect of changes in the rate of interest.

11.2   Simulation – an example

In this section we look at some of the simulation tests that were made on the original private sector equilibrium model. The structure of this model was fairly similar to the early versions of the 1955 – 70 model examined in Chapters 6, 7 and 8.[8] In order to make the model fully simulateable however it was necessary to linearise the variables in the demand equation so that the dependent variable was completions rather than completions per head and the monthly repayment variable was separated into two: price and the mortgage rate. The methods employed to provide these linear approximations were those described by Klein.[9] As a result the calculated coefficients apply only at the point of their means and so some bias is involved. However if this were not done there would be no basis for simulation as the price variable would be defined in a different way in the demand and supply equations and the completions variable in the demand and completions/starts equations.

The simulation experiments took two forms: (a) the simulation model was compared with actual data, and (b) the values of particular variables were changed and the results compared with the original simulated esti-mates.

Looking at the results of (a) we found that the simulated model moved in very similar ways to the actual data (see Chart 11.1 which shows the simulation demand for completions).[10] There was however a linear bias

153

because the results are very sensitive to the population coefficient. This is made up of the coefficients derived from the process of linearisation, a total of eight, all subject to considerable rounding error. This resulted in a stable error of about ten million on the population mean of about fifty-three million. Secondly, the simulated seasonal variation is greater than the actual in the first few years, also because of the linearisation around population mean. The seasonal dummies represent quarterly population calculated around the mean, but as population is actually an upward trend, the correction is too great in the early years. This bias from linearisation affects all equations, because after the initial period all the dependent variables are simultaneously determined through the interdependent equations. But in general the simulation results behave in a very similar way to the actual observations and it is therefore permissible to use them for analysing the effects of policy changes.

As an example of the effect of changes in policy we increased the supply rate of interest by 1 per cent in the first quarter and the mortgage rate by the same amount in the third quarter. [11]

The change in the rate of interest takes effect immediately and on average cuts back starts by 12·5 per cent each period. The effect on the supply of completions does not occur for another three quarters, because of the Koyck lag. [12]

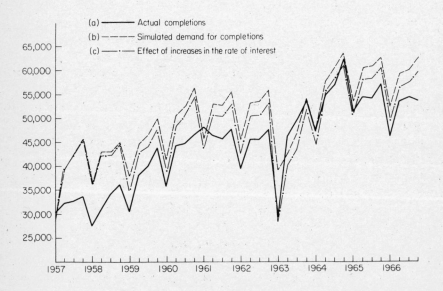

Fig. 11.1   Actual and simulated completions (with rate of interest changed)

Demand is affected by current price including mortgage costs which are changed in the third quarter, and the demand for completions then decreases in the third period by about 10 per cent (this is shown in Fig. 11.1). Demand is affected somewhat more than supply of completions and thus price drops very slightly, by less than 2 per cent. The effect on stock is cumulative. By the end of the eleven-year period of estimation 200,000 fewer dwellings are available as a result of the 1 per cent change in the rate of interest. [13]

From this experiment we conclude that both demand and supply are strongly affected by financial variables. A 1 per cent change of this type decreases both supply and demand by similar amounts. Therefore the price increase, resulting from increasing costs, is offset by the decrease in price as a result of decreased demand. However, far fewer dwellings are provided, and if there was excess *need* before the policy change, that situation would get worse. From the point of view of market price the changes in supply and demand have little effect. From the point of view of social policy the resultant decline in new building could be of extreme importance. Effective demand *and* supply are easily decreased (or increased by decreasing the rate of interest) resulting in a significant decline in the additions to stock.

11.3   The 1955 − 70 model

We have used the simulation of the 1955 − 66 model as an example because its rather simple format and method of estimation made it particularly suitable for simulation purposes. The models that we have been analysing in this book covering the periods 1955 − 70 and 1955 − 72 are more complex and simulation tests are as a result much less relevant. There are three properties of these models which cause difficulties.

First, in the 1955 − 66 model the effect of inflation (which had been running at much lower levels during that period than since 1966) was included via the rate of change of wholesale prices, rather than the rate of change of housing prices. Thus house prices, the equilibrating variable, entered simply having a negative effect on demand and a positive effect on supply. The model was therefore stable throughout the period (although the equilibrating assumption did cause the simulated price variable to vary much more than actual prices because in actuality vacancies often change in the short-run rather than prices). In the demand equations with the highest explanatory power over the 1955 − 70 period the rate of change of house prices was included as an independent variable and the coefficient had a positive sign. When linearised this means that two variables with the same coefficient enter the demand equation: aP_t with a positive sign and aP_{t-1} with a negative sign. The effect of a price change is therefore to increase demand immediately and to reduce it in the next period. The negative effect of the absolute level of house prices usually does not enter until period $t-2$. The size of this coefficient is large enough to outweigh the positive effect of P_t and the model is certainly stable in the long-run. But in the short-run the specification of P_t, P_{t-1} and P_{t-2} is likely to produce cycles especially as P_t and P_{t-1} are affected by upward linearisation bias in the early periods.

This results in a simulated price greater than actual price increasing supply and in the very short-run demand. The nature of the lag structure means that the simulation process cannot correct itself quickly and the results are therefore not very close to the actual observations of the endogenous variables. To remove this problem, which is inherent in the simulation process, more accurate specification of the lagged relationships especially between demand, prices and the rate of change of prices would be necessary. This is extremely difficult particularly because available house price data is not very accurate quarter to quarter and because the linearisation process necessary for simulation automatically produces bias.

A second difficulty arises because of the different specifications of the completions/starts lag structure between the 1955 − 66 model and the others. In the original model a Koyck distributed lag of the form $a + bPS_{t-3} + cPC_{t-1}$ was used and as the coefficient on PC_{t-1} was quite large and significant the structure was relatively stable. In the later versions the rational lag form:

$$a + bPS_{t-1} + cPS_{t-2} + dPS_{t-3} + ePS_{t-4} + fPS_{t-5} + gPS_{t-6}$$

was found to have higher explanatory power. This however means that any misspecification of the supply side is rapidly reflected in the price equation and therefore quickly affects the stability of the model. We have argued that the many supply side data problems imply that the starts equation is still poorly specified and so it is possible that important errors will be built into the simulation system. Furthermore the model is very sensitive to the seasonal coefficients and it is probable that these have varied somewhat over the estimation period.

Finally in the 1955 − 70 and 1955 − 72 models it was felt to be of particular importance to remove the autoregressive error. This was found to be significant in both the completions/starts and the starts equations. The resultant model reflects the underlying effect on the structure of the private new housing market of the specified independent variables rather

156

than coefficients including autoregressive error. The overall explanatory power is not complete because some variables are excluded, particularly because of lack of data. Also it is probable that there is some misspecification of the included variables because of multicollinearity and inadequate determination of the lag structure. Unless we were able to correct all these omissions it would not be possible to simulate the full model accurately. In a trend-filled world the inclusion of the autoregressive error, as in the 1955 − 66 model, is likely to produce a better approximation to actuality than a not fully complete structural model. It will certainly be better for forecasting purposes. In examining the effect of policies the structural model is far preferable but requires further analysis before full simulation is viable. All relevant variables must be correctly specified and this, unhappily, is not yet possible at the stage in housing model building which we have reached.

For all the above reasons results of the type described in relation to the 1955 − 66 model, although of interest, should be treated with great care. At this stage in our examination of the housing market we think it far more important to attempt to specify the model as correctly as possible, even if it is still incomplete rather than to use the existence of autoregressive error and simpler formulations, especially of the demand equation and the lag structure, to obtain apparently good simulation and forecasting results. These could not stand under deeper examination as we know that we have not been able to capture all the factors which affect the private new housing market. At this pilot stage it is better to concentrate on carefully specified partial relationships than to put forward an apparently complete system which has in fact important omissions. In the final chapter we discuss these problems, what can be done about them in the future and the uses, particularly in relation to the analysis of policy, to which the results obtained in this monograph can be of assistance.

Notes

[1] See A. Ando and F. Modigliani, 'Economic Analysis of Stabilisation Policies', *American Economic Review*, May 1969, p. 297. 'In the process of simulation solutions at each point of time and over time (through lagged dependent variables) there will be an opportunity for the single equation's errors to interact with each other and to be magnified as they pass through other equations of the system.'

[2] I. Adelman and F. Adelman, 'The Dynamic Properties of the Klein-Goldberger model', *Econometrica*, vol. 27, no. 4, October 1959. J. Duesenberry, O. Eckstein and G. Fromm, 'A Simulation of the United States Economy in Recession', *Econometrica*, vol. 28, no. 4, October 1960.

[3] G. Fromm and P. Taubman, *Policy Simulations with an Econometric Model,* The Brookings Institute, North-Holland Publishing Co., Amsterdam 1968.

[4] L. B. Smith, 'A Model of the Canadian Housing and Mortgage Markets', *Journal of Political Economy*, vol. 77, no. 5, September/October 1969. The model consisted of demand and starts equations for the housing market including a distributed lag structure for changes in stock. To this he added explanatory equations determining construction costs and the costs and availability of credit. He found many of the same data difficulties which occur in the UK (e.g. there was no acceptable vacancy series). The objection to his model lies mainly in that he was unable to separate the supply and demand factors involved in the costs of credit. This resulted in the starts equation being a reduced form rather than the structural equation necessary for the true formulation of the model. Simulation was mainly used to check the efficacy of the model. One shot changes in the rate of interest were tried but the results were somewhat ambiguous as a result of the poorly formulated starts equation.

[5] D. S. Huang and M. D. McCarthy, 'Simulation of the Home Mortgage Market in the Late Sixties', *Review of Economics and Statistics*, vol. 49, no. 4, November 1967.

[6] F. de Leeuw, and E. Gramlich, *The Federal Reserve – MIT Econometric Model*, Federal Reserve Bulletin, January 1968.

[7] M. J. Desai, 'An Econometric Model of the World Tin Economy – 1948 – 61', *Econometrica*, vol. 34, no. 1, January 1966.

[8] A full description of this model can be found in Appendix B, and further analysis of the results obtained and comparisons with other models is given in C. M. E. Whitehead, 'A Model of the UK Housing Market', *Bulletin of the Oxford University Institute of Economics and Statistics*, vol. 33, no. 4, 1971.

[9] L.R. Klein, *A Textbook of Econometrics*, Row Peterson & Co., Evanston 1956, p. 121.

[10] Other results showing the effect on starts, price, etc. can be found the author's PhD thesis, 'Some Aspects of the Economics of Housing in the UK', unpublished, University of London, 1970.

[11] The model is symmetric and thus the results would be exactly inverted if the interest rate had beeen reduced by 1 per cent.

[12] Here the cut-back is only in the region of 10 per cent as the Koyck distributed lag does not add to one.

[13] As this is just an example we have only included one chart, showing the effect on demand for completions. The other variables are affected in a similar way.

12   Future Trends in the Housing Market

12.1   Introduction

In this monograph we have discussed one possible model of the new housing market and set the assessment of this model against the background of more descriptive analysis of the current housing situation and the economic and other factors which have, over the century, led to this position. In the final chapter we attempt to bring the strands of discussion together and in the light of the available evidence examine the likely behaviour of the housing market over the next few years. We will concentrate particularly on some possible variations in government policy which may cause structural changes in the behaviour of the housing market.

It is important before embarking on this analysis to realise that the econometric model of the new housing market, which is the main part of this monograph, cannot be expected to provide full answers to questions about how the market will react to policy and other changes in determining variables. It is of course possible to extend the type of analysis discussed in Chapter 11 and from this in the end to obtain quantitative estimates, in terms of new house prices, number of completions and starts, of the effect of say reducing the mortgage rate of interest. But such answers are at best of limited use. They suggest which changes are likely to be important and which are not, they predict the direction of change and one would perhaps to this extent have faith in them. But the model would also predict the magnitude of the change in the dependent variables and their timing within specified margins of error. Here we would be very much less prepared to accept the answers obtained without further independent evidence.

The reasons for this uncertain attitude towards predictions obtainable from models of the type discussed in this monograph are numerous. They include:

1   The tested model includes only a very small number of independent variables. It is therefore probable that some of these are serving

as proxies for a number of other variables all of which may not always vary together especially when policy changes take place. One of the reasons for the small number of independent variables is the lack of available data — so there is little that can be done about it until better series (especially relating to land costs and vacancies) can be obtained.

2   The model specified is in linear form but there is little independent evidence to suggest that consumers and producers react to changes in independent variables in this way. We would not necessarily expect for instance that consumers would react to a jump in the rate of inflation from 10 per cent to 20 per cent by exactly ten times the amount they react to a change from 5 per cent to 6 per cent. Yet the model assumes this. We would perhaps expect instead that there is some threshold effect — that, for instance, consumers react to small changes in the inflation rate in a well-defined manner, but when the rate changes by more than X per cent they react in a totally different way (say by consuming far more rather than saving). These non-linear responses cannot easily be dealt with in econometric models, although it may be possible ex-post to examine reactions (if not more than one variable has changed at the same time) by analysing the residuals. Non-linear response is one possible reason for the difficulties encountered in examining the behaviour of the housing market in 1971 and 1972 when very large, and to some extent unexpected, changes took place in the housing market.

3   The lag structure specified in the model is extremely simple and because of the trend aspects of many of the variables it is quite likely that one cannot differentiate by the tests available between a number of possible lag structures. The lag between starts and completions does seem relatively stable but even then there is some evidence of variation in reaction to changes particularly in demand. This can only be analysed further with the help of extra observations and particularly with evidence on vacancy rates. On the demand side tests on lags on price and on the mortgage rate suggested that reaction is not always best explained by a two-period lag. In practice different consumers respond at different speeds to any change so a fully correct analysis would probably include distributed lag reactions on most variables. This would reflect true behaviour more precisely but it would also make the model unwieldy and degrees of freedom would soon run out. The lag reactions specified in the model are therefore only approximations at best.

4   The model specified is an equilibrium one where price equates demand and supply (taking into account the distributed lag) at the beginning and end of each quarter. Of course demand and supply are both defined as responding to lagged values of some of the independent variables but it is still a pretty heroic assumption. Some may argue that prices in the new housing market are pretty flexible and so can be expected to change so as to bring demand and supply into equilibrium each quarter. Others would say that to a great extent this process is accomplished more by changes in the vacancy rate of near completions than by changes in price. In this case suppliers probably fix prices on a cost plus basis when they start building an estate and do not vary price upwards if a few more consumers wish to buy than there are houses, or downwards unless the houses remain unsold for some time. The evidence of 1971 to 1973 when the market was booming certainly suggests that when prices are rising very rapidly many builders are prepared to 'gazump' buyers if others offer considerably more money but the fuss that this caused suggests that it is not altogether a normal process. Moreover when the market tightened in late 1973 and 1974 although there were signs of some price reductions and special offers (of e.g. colour televisions as a gift from the builder on completion or help with the mortgage) there was certainly an increase in the number of completed unsold houses. Indeed the government has allocated money specifically to local authorities to purchase these dwellings, of which there were said to be about 30,000 in April 1974.

Evidence of this type suggests that the equilibrium assumption is very much an oversimplification (although the fact that the model is quarterly rather than say monthly may mean that it is not too far out). Moreover when the model was first simulated for the period 1955–66 it was found that the assumption caused large variations in price which were not observed. This is not conclusive evidence because the model could well have been incorrectly specified in other ways but it is a further indication that the market is not entirely wellbehaved. To modify the model so that the importance of the assumption could be assessed would require vacancy data and the specification of a disequilibrium model which could be used for comparison, and perhaps prediction.[1]

5   This model of the housing market is only a partial analysis of the problem. In particular there is no model of the housing finance market which would be a necessary input into an overall model of how

the housing sector reacts to change. On the supply side a model of the construction industry's decision processes would also be necessary, especially if it were desired to use quantitative models for short-term forecasting purposes. A particular problem that we cannot solve by analysing this model is how the mortgage rate is related to the general rate of interest. For instance does the mortgage rate follow behind the general rate? Does it move by as much and is the reaction to downward movements symmetric with response to increases? Until we can model the structure of interest rates we will not be able to assess fully the problems of lagged supply response to demand changes brought about as a result of variations in the price and availability of finance. We cannot therefore say how prices will change because of this lagged response.

6   Finally because it is a partial and simple model the effects of many policy changes will only be reflected in the model indirectly and others not at all. This means that most policy variations will cause structural changes in the behaviour of the model and this in turn causes changes in the magnitude of the coefficients. An example is the effect of varying tax relief on mortgage interest. As tax relief is not specifically included in the mortgage rate (partly because it affects different people differently) the coefficient will change if there is any variation. If, say, relief were withdrawn the rate of interest that most house purchasers pay would increase but as the nominal rate would not the actual effect in the model would be to change the size of the coefficient on the interest rate variable. In order to analyse the effects of most policies, which act in a complex manner, it would be necessary to build far more sophisticated models and however many variables were included it would still be necessary to use judgement in interpreting the results.

These and other aspects of the model are reasons why this particular model can only be regarded as a pilot attempt in an extremely complex area. Some of the problems could be solved by building more sophisticated structures, others by obtaining more relevant time-series data. But it must be remembered that the housing market is more affected than most by administrative and political behaviour and therefore any quantitative model of feasible size is unlikely ever to be able to take into account all important external influences. Certainly as far as is known there is at the moment no model of the housing market in any western country which is usable on its own for predictive purposes. However models have been built in both the USA and Canada which provide forecasts which can be used to aid decisions in a fairly general manner.[2] Undoubtedly quantitative housing models even of the over-simple type described in this paper can help judgement, and so further work on data collection, theoretical analysis and empirical testing is likely to be worthwhile.

Yet any model is only as good as its assumptions and the complexity of the housing market makes it extremely difficult to analyse quantitatively. This is particularly true when massive changes are taking place in the whole working of the economy and in government policy towards housing. Since 1970 changes in the rate of inflation, in house prices and in rates of interest have been greater than anyone alive in Britain today has ever experienced before. As a result both consumers and producers have reacted in a very different way from normal. Quantitative models can help to indicate the nature of these reactions but in times of great change we cannot hope that they will be completely accurate.

When we examine the current housing situation and likely changes in the market and government policy towards housing the limitations of the model discussed above mean that we can only use its results as qualitative evidence in support of our predictions and analysis. This should be borne in mind throughout this chapter when we examine some possible changes in the housing market.

12.2   Possible changes in the housing market

The enormous structural changes in the housing market and in the overall economy have put the institutional framework and the whole working of the housing sector under stress. The most important causes are the very rapid increase in the rate of inflation, the resultant changes in interest rates and the desirability of owning assets whose prices rise at least at the same rate as inflation. This has affected not only the demand for housing and the price and availability of demand finance but also the costs and difficulties of building new dwellings. Further it has been found impossible to modify the administrative and financing structures of the local authority sector to take account of these changes quickly and public sector building programmes have been greatly reduced as a result.

The current stagnation in the new private housing market is seen as being an amalgam of three interacting factors: the decline of the net flow of funds into building societies, rapidly increasing mortgage rates and a decline in the number of private housing starts. The slowing down in the increase in availability of new finance over the last year (coupled with the enormous increase in house prices in 1971−73) has led to a mortgage famine which is expected to get worse. Indeed the net flow of new deposits less withdrawals to building societies was actually negative in March and April 1974. The cause of this decline is seen as the reduced competitiveness of building society interest rates to savers against rates paid by other financial institutions available to the small saver and against consumption as interest rates in general fall further behind the inflation rate. At the moment the building society saver receives about 7·5 per cent net of tax, roughly half the current inflation rate. The government is attempting to deal with this by lending the building societies £100 million per month for five months on the understanding that interest rates are held down. In this way they hope to keep up the availability of mortgage funds without further interest rate rises.

Table 12.1

Building societies' financial status 1971−74

	(1)	(2)	(3) = (1) + (2)	(4)	(5)
	Receipts of principal *less* withdrawals (£m.)	Interest credited to accounts (£m.)	Net increase in shares and deposits (£m.)	Repayment of mortgage principal (£m.)	Liquidity ratio
1971					
1st Quarter	330	64	394	220	17·6
2nd Quarter	367	86	453	284	17·9
3rd Quarter	454	69	523	318	18·2
4th Quarter	549	115	664	336	19·1
1972					
1st Quarter	503	76	519	304	18·3
2nd Quarter	475	99	574	354	17·9
3rd Quarter	359	80	439	388	16·6
4th Quarter	464	137	601	388	16·5
1973					
1st Quarter	321	95	416	377	14·4
2nd Quarter	595	146	741	394	15·8
3rd Quarter	321	117	438	427	15·9
4th Quarter	245	232	477	406	16·3
1974					
January	19	104	123	112	15·2

Source: *Financial Statistics*, No. 142, February 1974, Table 68.

Yet the crisis is not altogether one of declining supply of funds. The value of new shares and deposits continues to increase, roughly doubling between the end of 1970 and the end of 1973. But at the same time withdrawals have trebled, reducing the net availability to building societies until in March and April 1974 it became negative. The overall net flow of funds has not declined so drastically because this includes interest on earlier deposits not withdrawn. Further new mortgage availability depends not just on these two factors but also on repayments of principal which have been increasing fairly rapidly. (These are all shown in Table 12.1.) Against this however the average size of a mortgage has increased very greatly as house prices have gone up and so although the value of mortgage advances has not declined very much the number issued has gone down by about one third from the high point of the boom (Table 12.2). Many potential house buyers have been finding it extremely difficult to obtain a mortgage and the number of unsold new houses has been increasing.

Some of the current gloom results from the enormous success that the building societies have had in attracting funds in the late 1960s and early 1970s. Even the 1974 decline in mortgage advances is therefore only a reduction in comparison to one of the best periods ever for building societies. During that period the societies attracted something in the order of 60 per cent of all new personal savings to fuel this expansion in advances, a share that has risen from about 15–20 per cent in the mid-1950s. This massive expansion in the number of savers and the quantity of funds which was in general immediately lent out again has made the societies very vulnerable to sudden outflows of funds. The possibility is made more likely by the very fact of having attracted so much new money and by the societies' extraordinarily easy withdrawal regulations. Further the change in banking policy in 1971 caused competition to increase in the finance market as a whole and both the banking and other financial institutions have been able to offer higher returns than building societies to savers fearful of the consequences of inflation. There have thus been very considerable strains placed on the administrative and financial structures of the building societies of a type which are unlikely to be removed in the short run.[3] The solution requires not only a decline in the rate of inflation relative to the rate of interest but also either a reduction in the demand for housing finance or new sources of supply.[4]

The model that we have analysed throughout this monograph suggests that the flow of funds itself is only one of a number of factors determining the demand for new houses of which the most important variables are the price and the nominal rate of interest that purchasers have to pay. As both have risen very considerably in the last two years we might expect to find that the demand for new houses falls off against higher costs to the purchaser and therefore the availability of funds is perhaps not so much of a constraint as is currently being suggested. The only opposing factor is the increase in demand brought about by higher rates of inflation in general and house prices in particular, which appears to make houses a relatively more acceptable asset. What evidence there is from the period 1970–72 and the comparisons between the effect of general inflation and the increase in house prices suggests that purchasers are, if anything, becoming more precautionary. Yet this quantitative evidence is extremely

Table 12.2

Value and number of mortgage advances 1971–74

	Value of mortgage advances (£m.)	Average advance (£)	Number of mortgage advances (thousands)
1971			
1st Quarter	509	3803	134
2nd Quarter	677	3968	166
3rd Quarter	786	4187	183
4th Quarter	786	4363	177
1972			
1st Quarter	769	4644	163
2nd Quarter	925	4987	181
3rd Quarter	1020	5497	181
4th Quarter	935	5636	165
1973			
1st Quarter	967	5997	159
2nd Quarter	855	6054	138
3rd Quarter	891	6274	141
4th Quarter	734	NA	113
1974			
January	221	NA	34

Sources: *Financial Statistics*, No. 142, February 1974, Table 70. *Housing and Construction Statistics*, No. 7, third quarter, 1973, Table VIII.

limited if one wishes to build future policy upon it. Since the end of 1972 the rate of inflation has doubled and at the same time the rate of return available both on the stock market and in fixed interest securities has relatively declined. House prices although not necessarily keeping pace with inflation have certainly done better than most other assets and, as we have argued before, housing is the only hedging asset that the individual can relatively easily borrow money to buy. The behaviour of the model in 1970–72 may well reflect uncertainty in the face of unexpected inflation and it is perhaps likely that this will be overcome as higher rates of inflation become more probable. There would then be an increase in demand even at going house prices. This seems even more likely as real rates of interest are held down by government policy. At the moment the net rate that mortgagors pay, if standard taxpayers, is 7·64 per cent against an inflation rate of almost 15 per cent. Over and above this, house prices more than kept pace with inflation up to the end of 1973. Therefore, taking account of the structural change in the rate of inflation and the lagged reaction of consumers, the evidence suggests that there is probably suppressed demand for houses at the present time as the availability of funds has declined against increasing money incomes while rates of interest are being held below their equilibrium level.

The effect of increasing the flow of funds to building societies will be to make this excess demand effective but how the funds are obtained is of great importance. If the increased flow of funds occurs because societies wish, and are permitted, to increase the rates of interest to attract more savings (and more importantly slow down withdrawals) then the rising rate of interest will itself dampen demand. But if the expansion of funds results from government reallocating funds to building societies (as the current £100 million per month scheme does) without raising the rate of interest demand will not be reduced and may even increase consequent on the expectation of further help to house purchase. In this case unless supply can be expanded very rapidly as the funds become available, house prices are likely to rise as demand becomes effective against an inelastic supply.

The effectiveness of such policies to aid the expansion of home ownership must therefore rest upon the behaviour of supply in the new housing market. New private starts never quite rose during the 1972–73 boom as high as in 1967, when 233,000 dwellings were started. Still, over 227,000 were started in 1972. After the fourth quarter of 1972 however starts began to fall again and in the fourth quarter of 1973 they were more than 25 per cent below the final quarter of the year before. This decline has continued into 1974.

Our model is inadequately detailed, especially on the supply side, to do more than indicate possible reasons for this decline and to examine qualitatively likely reactions to changes in the independent variables. We would expect the decline to be the result of increases in the cost of supply finance and other costs of production (especially as house prices have continued to rise faster than other prices) rather than being particularly related to the decline in the flow of funds to building societies. This should have some effect but the model suggests that it is not more than, at the most, 2,000 units per quarter while we are looking for an explanation for a decline of more than 10,000.

Looking at the cost of finance to builders we find that the minimum lending rate started to rise in October 1972, fell somewhat during the first half of 1973 and increased again quite rapidly thereafter. This suggests that the rising cost of finance could well have been an important factor in the decline of new activity. Moreover land prices continued to rise at least until the third quarter of 1973. Perhaps the most important factor on the supply side was the massive increase in the amount of house improvement work undertaken. This sometimes requires almost as much skilled labour as in new building but it has a fairly certain rate of profit and does not require so much finance on the part of the builder. In times of uncertainty many builders might move into this area so putting up the costs of labour for new construction and reducing its availability. Thus the massive increase in government aid to house improvement (in both the private and public sectors) may well be as much or more a cause of the decline in private new construction as the uncertainty of mortgage finance or even the cost of supply finance. The figures are given in Table 12.3 and it should be remembered that there is probably at least a quarter's lag before the work is actually done.[5]

If these other factors, which, the model suggests, might well be more important than the effect of demand finance, continue to affect supply then attempting to solve the problems of the new private housing market by increasing demand finance will not have any very great influence on expanding supply. The most likely result will be a rise in house prices. This should cause an increase in private starts but it may be offset by further rises in land prices unless government policies towards land such as nationalisation are able to force land prices down again.

In the immediate future there is little expectation of an expansion in the private housing market. While rates of interest are held down for house purchasers demand finance cannot be expected to come from the normal finance market. Indeed continuing government help will be required if the building societies are not to lose further funds. On the supply

170

side, however, rates of interest have increased and are continuing to do so. This together with increases in other construction costs is not likely to give the builder the incentive to build unless other possible outlets for their work close.

If ultimately both demand and supply interest rates rise in line with inflation on the basis of the model's results demand will be cut back but also supply. Indeed in the 1955—66 simulation described in Chapter 11 an equal change in demand and supply rates was shown to have a slightly greater effect on demand than on supply. Moreover demand rates, because they have not kept pace with inflation, are likely, in the absence of further government intervention, to rise by a larger amount than supply rates. Demand will therefore be further reduced to meet the declining available supply. On the other hand many people who have bought houses in the last two years and others buying now while the government is controlling interest rates may find themselves with considerable cash flow problems. The government may then feel that they must give short-term assistance particularly to first-purchasers.[6] If, in the longer run, rates more closely reflect inflation far more radical changes in the mortgage structure either through 'indexing' or by giving savers (or possibly the financial institutions) part of the equity will probably have to be considered.

The results of our general analysis, and particularly those which can be derived from the model, suggest that any action to assist demand is not

Table 12.3

Improvement grants approved, Great Britain

	For private owners	For local authorities	For housing associations	Total
1968	84,860	40,939	2,096	127,895
1969	80,263	40,436	3,190	123,889
1970	116,379	59,468	4,110	179,957
1971	137,364	88,979	6,168	232,511
1972	224,468	136,844	6,756	368,068
1973	First 3 quarters only			
	196,138	141,798	4,030	341,966

Source: *Housing and Construction Statistics*, No. 7, third Quarter, 1973, Table 28.

171

likely to expand supply greatly because of the lags in construction, and the relative effects of interest rates and prices on demand and supply. If the economy as a whole desires more new housing then action must be taken directly on the supply side either by expanding public sector provision or by assisting the private builder. Here there seem to be two extremely important factors: finance and land prices.

If any increase in house prices or reduction in costs to builders is automatically taken up by increases in land prices there will never be any expansion in supply as a result of changes in these variables. Builders will earn normal profit, will go elsewhere when above normal profits can be earned in other types of construction and return to house building when other possibilities dry up. Thus the hypothesis of infinitely inelastic supply of land has extremely important policy implications and attempts should be made to test it before policies affecting other variables are put into operation.[7]

The model tested in this monograph is of little use for analysing this hypothesis in depth. First it assumes that all the determining variables are independent of one another and therefore does not allow explicitly for any relationship between the price of land and the price of houses.

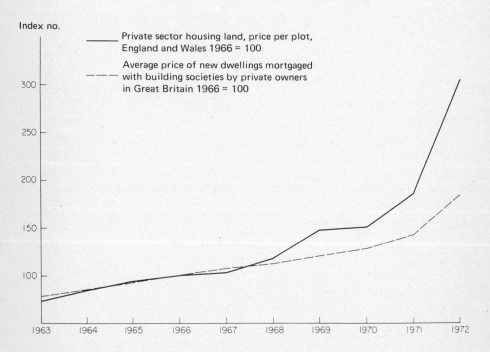

Fig. 12.1 New housing and land prices

Secondly the land data used is only a proxy variable and cannot hope to pick up all the interactions between the housing and land markets. The hypothesis that prices are very strongly related can be examined diagrammatically, of course, as is done in Fig. 12.1,[8] and this suggests that during the early part of the period for which data are available land and house prices moved very closely together. But after 1967 land prices increased far more rapidly perhaps suggesting that expectations of future house price increases (and future inflation) were already being incorporated into the land price.[9] To define the relationship in more detail however a quantitative model of the determination of land prices should be built and incorporated into the model of the new housing market. This has not been possible up to now because of the lack of available data but in the next few years sufficient should be available for a first attempt.

A priori, however, we would not expect the supply of housing land to be infinitely inelastic. Such an hypothesis requires that planning permission is completely unresponsive to changes in the demand for housing and that density regulations allow no flexibility in the number of housing units built on a plot. Neither of these assumptions seems likely although detailed studies should be attempted to discover the extent of any flexibility. Even if there is some elasticity of supply of land, however, the length of the supply lag for houses is long enough for most short-term measures aiding demand to result in increased house prices which will increase profits to both the builder and the land developer (as the supply of land is certainly not infinitely elastic). If the objective is to build more homes without increasing prices to the consumer, relaxation of controls or direct subsidies to builders before there is any assistance in expanding demand is more likely to be effective.

Any increase in the availability of land for house building should decrease land prices and increase the profitability to builders — and against a given demand structure therefore reduce house prices. The easiest way of obtaining this result would be to ease planning permission and to reduce the administrative, legal and other costs of obtaining such permission. The supply of land would then be increased and more importantly expectations that more land would continue to be available would be built up: the gains from land hoarding would therefore decline. There might of course be costs to such action in that extra development possibly at higher density levels may result in external costs to those who already reside in the area. These costs should be measured and weighed against the long-term provision of more houses at lower direct cost. Land nationalisation is one way of going about increasing the supply as long as the rules for freeing land for development are slackened as a result. The short-term effect however is almost certain to be in the opposite direction in that uncertainties about the future are likely to slow down the process of giving planning permission.

Making more land available or changing densities is a necessary condition for building more houses. But even so if there are constraints in terms of the cost and availability of finance and other factors of production especially skilled labour all that will happen, at least in the short-run, is that builders will make higher profits and few extra houses will be built. Policy therefore should also be directed at increasing the availability of these factors if expansion in output is required. In particular there might well be assistance in terms of increasing the availability of credit to builders concentrating especially on stabilising this availability. This might well involve some kind of guarantee system because builders' difficulties in obtaining funds probably arise mainly because they are such high-risk firms. Alternatively, or as a supplementary policy, incentives could be offered to try and increase the overall stability of house-building firms. This would probably entail increasing the capital output ratio and so would require changes in building methods. Such modifications could be assisted by varying some of the building society rules relating to house structures particularly those which work against building flats instead of houses and against the use of non-traditional materials.

There are many other important trends in the housing field, but a large proportion of the short-term problems relate to the relative ease of varying demand in comparison with the difficulties of expanding supply. The solution undoubtedly does not lie solely in increasing the availability of funds either to purchasers or to suppliers but requires more complex measures which take account of the long lags in reaction particularly on the supply side and the interrelationship between the housing market, the land market, the overall finance market and the level of economic activity.

12.3 Further research work

The model that has been discussed in this paper is extremely simple and can only be seen as a pilot study on the basis of which further work might be undertaken. The problems in continuing are of two types: data requirement and structural complexities.

Although since 1966 there has been an enormous increase in the quality and quantity of data available there are still very large gaps which make it difficult to build any full-scale model of the housing market. Moreover

174

some of the most important series have not been collected for long enough to be of much use as yet.

The lack of adequate data is most important on the supply side. There is now a series on land prices but although it starts in 1966 the basis of it has been changed since and furthermore it is estimated on a six-monthly basis. The change in its structure is that pre-1969 the index reflected price per plot at current density while it is now estimated on a constant average density basis. As we have argued that one of the relevant variables is the effect on density of changes in land prices this modification is particularly important. Perhaps most important however is the enormous variation in land prices across the country which means that the make-up of the sample may affect the value of a given observation far more than any underlying change in price. Ideally we would like two series one giving land prices per acre and another trends in density but there would still be great difficulty in determining the lag structure. Moreover the relatively small and variable number of transactions means that a quarterly series would be subject to large margins of error. These problems are inherent in the nature of the land market and we cannot hope that a single index will adequately reflect all the complexities. [10] Perhaps one way round the difficulty would be an extensive cross-section study of the land market which would enable us to determine certain relationships such as the effect of density of building on changes in the price of land. Such coefficients could be used as inputs into a modified new housing market model.

Another data problem on the supply side is in relation to construction, particularly labour, costs. Rather than simply using the price of building materials and wage rates it would be more relevant to deflate these by indices of productivity change. [11] While the measures of the number of workers in the industry are affected by 'the lump' it is unlikely that an accurate estimate of productivity change can be obtained. It might be possible to analyse indirect evidence available from local authority contracts over time, but it is certain that a full time -series index could not be determined. [12] Alternatively it would be difficult but worthwhile to try and obtain direct evidence on builders' profits although there would be considerable valuation problems, particularly in relation to land values. Again it is unlikely that such evidence could be built into a time-series model but it would provide further relevant evidence on the behaviour of builders.

The third area of data deficiency is related to house builders' finance. We have argued that cost and availability of supply finance are important factors in the housing market but the indicators employed are far from satisfactory. The most useful series would be the supply of bank funds to house builders in particular, rather than to the construction industry in general. Further it would be very important to have a cost of finance series which took into account the riskiness of house building and any variation in costs that this entails. It might well be necessary to survey builders at regular intervals to discover their situation relative to the rest of the economy.

Finally on the supply side there is the problem of the house price index. Until now it has not been possible to use any series other than that provided by the Nationwide Building Society. This is rather biased because the society sometimes mortgages more than an average number of lower-priced dwellings. Since 1968 the Department of the Environment has published a series which covers dwellings mortgaged by all building societies but this is still incomplete because no evidence on dwellings mortgaged by insurance companies or local authorities is included and there is no information on dwellings bought without financial assistance. Because here we are interested in the price of new houses the most important exclusion is likely to be those mortgaged by insurance companies. The index is thus likely to be downward biased. As yet this index is not extensive enough to be used in time-series analysis but there is a case for substituting the Department's series as soon as there are enough observations.

The problem of a reliable price index is just as important on the demand side but otherwise data is generally of better quality here. It is unlikely that changes in household formation could ever be of great importance in determining short-term demand but it might be worthwhile to experiment with more sensitive series than population or marriages. The area where most improvement could be obtained relatively easily would be in relation to the finance market. The evidence about the relative importance of cost and availability of finance in determining demand in this model is not conclusive because the two measures of availability used (Spencer and O'Herlihy dummies and the net flow of funds) may well not be an adequate reflection of the behaviour of even the building society sector let alone the effect of substitute sources on the financing of house purchase. In order to deal with this problem properly a full model of building society behaviour would be required especially if independent evidence suggests that for long periods there is rationing of mortgages by building societies. Evidence on the number of applications compared with grants is not an adequate measure of the existence of excess demand because potential house purchasers may apply to a number of building societies and ultimately be satisfied. Certainly future work on possible indices of availability of credit to house purchase would enable more complex models of demand to be tested.

Perhaps the most important data deficiency is the lack of any series on vacancy rates either for existing or new dwellings. Without such a series it is not possible to build a model to test whether short-term adjustment takes place through variations in quantity rather than price and what effect the changes in the length of waiting between completion and sale have on new starts. The current evidence would, at first sight, suggest that builders are keeping up prices at the cost of holding completed dwellings for quite long periods, and at the same time new starts have declined very considerably. Vacancy data should help us to test this type of hypothesis about short-run behaviour and would also be necessary for any more complex structure of the model involving disequilibrium in the new housing market. At the moment some qualitative evidence can be obtained from the *Estates Gazette* but as supply is a priori expected to be sensitive to such a variable more precise information would be of great assistance. In the future a series could be obtained by surveying a sample of firms at regular intervals although this is likely to be a costly procedure because of the characteristics of the industry (especially the short life and variable levels of output of many firms). The best one could hope for from the past would be to construct a series of dummies based on the *Estates Gazette* evidence.

The difficulties of obtaining hard data in relation to the housing market means that at the present time sophisticated models would be out of place as they would assume an accuracy of information which does not really exist. However before a full understanding even of the new housing market can be obtained far more complex structural relationships must be tested. This will involve modelling other markets than that of new housing particularly the finance markets for both demand and supply, the land market and the behaviour of the existing housing market and its interaction with the market for new dwellings.

It is not necessary that analysis of all of these markets form a completely interlocking system. What is required in most cases is detailed examination of each individual market from which results can be fed into the basic model. It is perhaps most important to build a joint model between new housing and finance because the specification of the lag structure is so crucial.

In determining the relationship between the demand for new housing and the market for demand finance two hypotheses require particular attention at the present time. First, to what extent does the availability of finance constrain demand? [13] The evidence of the model put forward here is that societies do not completely control housing demand in such a way that there is always excess demand at current prices. Yet further analysis comparing behaviour between periods when there was felt to be considerable stress and when there was not would assist policy formulation greatly. Perhaps, given the current inflation and the apparent breakdown in the demand finance structure, it might be more immediately relevant to examine the relationship between building societies and other institutions that might provide finance for house purchase. If there has always been excess demand for mortgages in the post-war period it seems surprising that other institutions have not entered the market to a greater extent. This is particularly likely to occur in situations like the present when there is continuing talk of such excess demand and where housing, unlike the share market, has been one of the few areas where a full hedge against inflation can be obtained. As the structure of interest rates and expectations of inflation vary we would expect to find changes in the relationships between financial institutions, the methods of lending and the whole structure of the mortgage finance market. Some attempt to analyse the possible substitution effects between these institutions and the likely effect on the overall flow of funds would be of great assistance to policy.

We have already argued that a study should be made of the role of both supply and demand finance in determining the level and timing of housing starts. This can probably be done as a separate exercise from the full housing model and parameters from the first can then be included in the second. Particular emphasis should be placed on the nature of the lags between changes in the cost and availability of finance and the decision to start work, as in the short-run it is this lag which may be a major cause of house price increases. A related project which can be accomplished within the current framework of the model is to examine in more detail the extent to which the lag between start and completion is a function of economic variables.

Work to test the hypothesis that rising house prices are mainly passed on in increased land prices is probably of the most immediate importance if it is desired to expand new housing supply. With access to the raw data that makes up the land price index it might be possible to build a regional model although one could not expect to obtain entirely accurate results because of the data difficulties discussed above. But if land nationalisation is to go ahead and to have any effect on the housing market (other than to redistribute developers' profits) it is important to be far more clear as to the capacity of the building industry to expand supply, their reaction to increases in profits and whether there are any other binding constraints on builders' behaviour.

Finally, and perhaps most important if our aim is to meet social demand for housing, research should be undertaken on the effect of subsidies and taxes on the relative utility of owning versus renting and the comparative costs of producing private and public sector dwellings. The current government is going some way to reduce the relative benefit of ownership by removing mortgage interest relief from certain categories. It is possible that in time either this will be extended or capital gains tax on inputed income from home ownership introduced. At the same time council rents are being held down and there appears to be a movement towards decreasing the real costs of renting from the local authority. These changes will affect the tenure split demanded and should imply a move away from the private sector especially if mortgage interest rates increase to take correct account of inflationary pressures as they have not done over the last decade. Such a reversal will not necessarily reduce effective demand for new private dwellings in the short-run if at the moment there is excess demand. [14] But if the change persists there will be ultimately be some decline in this demand. [15] Any effect of this nature would make meeting the social end of increasing the overall housing stock very much more difficult to achieve. New building would come more and more from the public sector – and there is very little known about how local authorities make their decisions to build or not to build. [16] Research is therefore required on three fronts: (a) what is the socially optimal level of housing provision; (b) what is the socially optimal tenure split and (c) what affects the local authorities' decision to supply new dwellings.

The programme for further research set out in this section is vast, especially in comparison with what has been attempted until now. Yet if we wish to be able to answer basic questions such as what are the likely levels of housing starts, completions and prices next year and in five years time and what effect will particular government policies have on the new housing market analysis of the type suggested here is absolutely necessary. Further theoretical and statistical research is required and, within the second, models designed specifically for forecasting and for structural examination must be specified. It is unlikely that in the next few years fully satisfactory models will be forthcoming if only because of lack of data but even now proper specification is useful in forcing improvement of data sources. In this country only a start has so far been made but even from a simple model of the type presented here there are enough indicators to determine the direction of future work and to suggest that such research would be of very considerable value.

Notes

[1] A very simple disequilibrium model was tested for the 1955–66 period which simulated fairly well for the years under discussion. This assumed that changes in price rather than the absolute price level reflected supply and demand. There was no attempt because of lack of data to take account of quantity adjustment via variations in the vacancy rate. For a discussion of this model see C. M. E. Whitehead, 'A Model of the UK Housing Market', *Oxford Bulletin of Economics and Statistics*, vol. 33, no. 4, November 1971.

[2] For a discussion of these see F. de Leeuw and E. Gramlich, *The Federal Reserve – MIT Econometric Model*, Federal Reserve Bulletin, January 1968, pp. 11–40; J. H. Kalchbrenner, 'Summary of the Current Financial Intermediary Mortgage and Housing Sections of the FRB-MIT-PENN Econometric Model', paper presented at the Housing Model Conference for Federal Home Loan Bank Board, Washington DC, March 1971; and L. B. Smith, 'A Model of the Canadian Housing and Mortgage Markets', *Journal of Political Economy*, vol. 77, no. 5, September/October 1969.

[3] For a review of the importance of building societies within the financial and housing markets see J. Revell, 'UK Building Societies', *Economic Research Papers*, no. 5, University College of North Wales, Bangor 1973, and for an analytic but more out of date approach see J. Moreh, 'Aspects of Building Society Finance', unpublished PhD thesis, London University, 1967.

[4] There have been a very large number of articles putting forward explanations of possible ways of alleviating the current mortgage crisis. See for example, C. D. Foster and C. M. E. Whitehead 'Mortgages', *New Society*, 20 September 1973, and 'More Homes of Our Own', *New Society*, 14 March 1974; J. Black, 'A New System for Mortgages', *Lloyds Bank Review*, no. 111, January 1974; F. Hirsch, 'The Great Mortgage Morass and a Way Out', the *Guardian*, September 1973. A.W.J. Merrett and A. Sykes, *Housing Finance and Development: An analysis and programme for reform*, Longmans, London 1965.

[5] General analysis of the building industry can be found in M. E. A. Bowley, *The British Building Industry*, Cambridge University Press, Cambridge 1966, but specific information about the methods of choice between improvement and new building is not available.

[6] For a discussion of the possible ways of modifying the mortgage market to help such purchasers see M. Bromwich and C. M. E. Whitehead, *The Economic Consequences of the Mortgage Crisis*, forthcoming.

[7] The hypothesis was analysed in R. Turvey, *The Economics of Real Property*, Allen & Unwin, London 1957, but no empirical testing was possible. The availability of land in relation to urban development is also examined in descriptive term by P. A. Stone, *Urban Development in Britain: Standards, Costs and Resources 1964–2004*, vol. I, Cambridge University Press, Cambridge 1970, but the data available up to now has not been suitable for full-scale econometric model building.

[8] The figures are also given in Table 2.3.

[9] This is particularly likely as builders and developers attempt to build up land banks and often do not expect to use land they buy immediately.

[10] See A. W. Evans, 'Private Sector Housing Land Prices in England and Wales', *Economic Trends*, no. 244, February 1974, for a discussion of the basis of the current index and the available raw data.

[11] It would also be better to use earnings rather than wage data. This would require some modifications of the existing series as no quarterly consistent series exists for the whole period.

[12] Some work in this field has been done by the Building Research Establishment and by the Greater London Council.

[13] Since the first piece of published work on this subject by M. Wray, 'Building Society Mortgages and the Housing Market', *Westminster Bank Review*, February 1968, there have been many descriptive discussions of the relationship but up to now there has been little strictly relevant published econometric work.

[14] See C. M. E. Whitehead, 'Inflation and the New Housing Market', *Oxford Bulletin of Economics and Statistics*, vol. 35, no. 4, November 1973, for a more extensive discussion of housing market behaviour in inflationary periods.

[15] It should be remembered in forecasting future housing demand that the apparent inflation-proof nature of housing as an investment is not worldwide. In the United States and in Australia for instance house prices in the post-war period have rarely kept pace with inflation.

[16] See N. Topham, 'Housing Authorities and the Investment Decision', the *Manchester School*, December 1970, and R. J. Nicholson and N. Topham, 'Determinants of Investment in Housing by Local Authorities: An Econometric Approach', *Journal of the Royal Statistical Society Series A (General)*, vol. 134, part 3, 1971, for a discussion of possible ways of modelling local authority behaviour.

Appendices

Appendix A

Symbols and data sources

Symbols used

BC	Housebuilding materials
BSM	Building societies' mortgage rate of interest (i)
C	Completions
C*	Desired completions
CC	Construction costs defined as 60 per cent WR, 20 per cent BC, 20 per cent L
CR	Real construction costs i.e. CC/RPI
Ds	Seasonal dummies plus dummy for first quarter 1963
D_1, D_2, D_3	Dummies for quarters one, two and three
D_{63}	Dummy for first quarter 1963
DP	Rate of change of house prices $\dfrac{P_t - P_{t-1}}{P_{t-1}}$
DPR	Deflated rate of change of house prices
DW	Rate of change of retail prices $\dfrac{R_t - R_{t-1}}{R_{t-1}}$
FF	Net flow of funds into building societies
i	Mortgage rate of interest (BSM)
L	Land costs
MR	Medium rationing
N	Population
P	House prices
P*	Expected rate of inflation
PC	Private completions
PC/N	Private completions per head
PM	$Pi^t\left[\dfrac{1-t}{1-i^t}\right]$ i.e. the quarterly repayment when $t = 20$ years
PMR	Quarterly repayment deflated by retail price index
PR	House price index deflated by the retail price index
PS	Private starts

185

r	Rate of interest to builders
RPI	Retail price index
SR	Strong rationing
ST	Housing stock
ST^*	Desired level of housing stock
ST/N	Housing stock per capita
T	Time trend
WR	Construction industry wage rate
Y	Personal disposable income
Y/N	Personal disposable income per head
YR	Personal disposable income deflated by retail price index
YRP	Personal disposable income per head deflated by retail price index

In the tables a number of indicators are usually given:

r^2	Regression coefficient
$\overline{r}^{\,2}$	Corrected r^2
alpha 1	Coefficient of autocorrelation
DW	Durbin—Watson statistic
s	Standard error of the estimate

't' statistics are given in brackets beneath each coefficient

Data sources used in 1955—70 and 1955—72 models

Symbols	Variables	Unit	Data source
CC	Construction costs 60 per cent wages, 20 per cent house building materials, 20 per cent land	Index no. 1958 = 100	Wages (construction industry wage rate) house building materials. Land 2 per cent compound interest rates } *Monthly Digest of Statistics*, published monthly by the CSO
Ds	Seasonal dummies and dummy for first quarter of 1963	0 or 1	—
FF	Net flow of funds	£m.	*Financial Statistics* published monthly by CSO
i	Mortgage rate of interest	percentage rate per quarter	*Financial Statistics* published monthly by CSO
MR	Mild rationing	0 or 1	O'Herlihy and Spencer, 1971
N	Population	'000's	*Monthly Digest of Statistics*, published monthly by CSO; annual data interpolated linearly for quarters

186

P	Prices of new dwellings	Index no. 1958 = 100	Nationwide Building Society (prices of new dwellings mortgaged by the society)
PC	Private completions	No. of dwellings	*Housing and Construction Statistics*, published quarterly by Department of the Environment, Scottish Development Department and Welsh Office
PS	Private starts	No. of dwellings	*Housing and Construction Statistics*, published quarterly by Department of the Environment, Scottish Development Department and Welsh Office
r	Rate of interest	percentage rate per quarter	*Financial Statistics*, published monthly by CSO; gross flat yield on 2·5 per cent consols
RPI	Retail price index	Index no. 1958 = 100	*Monthly Digest of Statistics*, published monthly by CSO
SR	Strict rationing	0 or 1	O'Herlihy and Spencer, 1971
ST	Existing stock	'000's	*Housing and Construction Statistics*, published quarterly by Department of the Environment; annual data interpolated quarterly
Y	Total personal disposable income	£m.	*Economic Trends*, published monthly by CSO

Appendix B

The structure of the 1955–66 model

Demand equation:

$$PC/N_t = a + b\left(Y/N_t\right) - c\left(\frac{PM}{W} - DW\right) - d\left(W_t\right)$$
$$- e\left(ST/N_{t-1}\right) + f\left(PC/N_{t-1}\right) + Ds$$

Completions/Starts equation:

$$PC_t = g + h\,(PC_{t-1}) + j\,(PS_{t-3}) + Ds$$

Supply equation:

$$PS_t = k - l\,(r_{t-1}) + m\,(P_t) - n\,(CC_t) + o\,(T) + p\,(PS_{t-1}) + Ds.$$

The 1955–66 private sector equilibrium flow model

(a) $PC/N_t = 0{\cdot}23 + 9{\cdot}04\,(Y/N)t - 0{\cdot}06\left(\dfrac{\hat{P}M}{W} - DW\right)_t - 0{\cdot}004\,(W)_t$

$\qquad\qquad\quad (1{\cdot}85) \qquad\qquad (0{\cdot}02) \qquad\qquad\qquad\qquad (0{\cdot}002)$

$\qquad - 0{\cdot}00003\ \ (ST/N)_{t-1} + 0{\cdot}57\,(PC^D/N)_{t-1} + Ds$
$\qquad (0{\cdot}000014) \qquad\qquad\qquad (0{\cdot}09)$

$\qquad r^2 = 0{\cdot}964 \qquad DW = 1{\cdot}96 \qquad df\,32$

(b) $PC_t = 6503{\cdot}19 + 0{\cdot}75\,(PC)_{t-1} + 0{\cdot}18\,(PS)_{t-3} - Ds$

$\qquad\qquad\qquad\quad (0{\cdot}12) \qquad\qquad (0{\cdot}09)$

$\qquad r^2 = 0{\cdot}947 \qquad DW = 1{\cdot}62 \qquad df\,37$

(c) $PS_t = 195359{\cdot}13 - 5771{\cdot}35\,(r)_{t-1} + 221{\cdot}01\,(\hat{P})_t - 1672{\cdot}44\,(CC)_t$

$\qquad\qquad\qquad (1511{\cdot}51) \qquad\qquad (124{\cdot}71) \qquad\qquad (389{\cdot}10)$

$\qquad + 2772{\cdot}67\ T + 0{\cdot}28\,(PS)_{t-1} + Ds$
$\qquad (450{\cdot}01) \quad (0{\cdot}11)$

$\qquad r^2 = 0{\cdot}937 \qquad DW = 1{\cdot}53 \qquad df\,34$

(The figures in brackets refer to standard errors)
(^ indicates two-stage least-squares estimate)

Elasticities

Demand		*Supply*	
Income	0·99	Rate of interest	−0·71
Price and mortgage rate	−0·48	Construction costs	−5·02
		Price	0·62

Symbols used in 1955−66 model

CC   Construction costs: 60 per cent wages, 20 per cent building materials, 20 per cent land

Ds   Seasonal dummies plus dummy for first quarter 1963

DW $\dfrac{W_t - W_{t-1}}{W_{t-1}}$

i   Mortgage rate

N   Population

P   House prices

PC   Private completions

PM   House prices + mortgage rate $P(1 + i)^{20}$

PS   Private starts

r   Rate of interest in 2·5 per cent consols

ST   Total stock of housing

T   Time trend

W   Wholesale price index

Y   Personal disposable income four-quarter moving average

Data sources are normally as for the 1970 model: see Appendix A.

Bibliography

M. Abromovitz, *Evidence of the Long Swings in Aggregate Construction since the Civil War*, Princeton University Press for National Bureau of Economic Research, Princeton NJ 1964.

I.Adelman and F.Adelman, 'The Dynamic Properties of the Klein-Goldberger Model', *Econometrica*, vol. 27, no. 4, October 1959.

S.Almon, 'The Distributed Lag Between Capital Appropriations and Expenditures', *Econometrica*, vol. 33, January 1965, pp. 178–96.

A.Ando and F.Modigliani, 'Econometric Analysis of Stabilisation Policies', *American Economic Review Papers and Proceedings*, May 1969.

F.Arcelus and A.H.Meltzer, 'The Markets for Housing and Housing Services', *Journal of Money Credit and Banking*, vol. V, no. 1, pt 1, 1973.

R.J.Ball and T.Burns, 'The Prospects of Faster Growth in Britain', *National Westminster Bank Review*, November 1968.

V.L.Bassie, *Economic Forecasting*, McGraw-Hill, New York 1958.

J.Black, 'A New System for Mortgages', *Lloyds Bank Review*, no. 111, January 1974.

M.E.A.Bowley, *Housing and the State 1919–44*, Allen & Unwin, London 1945.

M.E.A.Bowley, *The British Building Industry: Four Studies in Response and Resistance to Change*, Cambridge University Press, Cambridge 1966.

C.F.Break, *The Economic Impact of Federal Loan Insurance*, National Planning Association, Washington DC 1961.

M. Bromwich and C.M.E. Whitehead, 'The Economic Consequences of the Mortgage Crisis', *The Accountant* vol. 171, no. 5193, 4 July 1974.

E.H. Phelps Brown and J. Wiseman, *A Course in Applied Economics* (2nd ed.), Pitman, London 1965.

I.C.R.Byatt, A.E.Holmans and D.Laider, 'Income and the Demand for Housing: Some Evidence for Great Britain' in M.Parkin (ed.), Association of University Teachers in Economics Conference, Aberystwyth 1972, *Essays in Modern Economics*, Longmans, London 1973.

University of California, *Essays in Urban Land Economics* in honour of the sixty-fifth birthday of Leo Grebler, Real Estate Research Program, Los Angeles 1966.

J.Carmichael, 'Vacant Possession', *Institute of Economic Affairs Hobart Papers*, the Institution, London 1964.

C.F.Carter and A.D.Roy, *British Economic Statistics: A Report*, Cambridge University Press, Cambridge 1954.

J.B.Cullingworth, *Housing Needs and Planning Policy*, Routledge & Kegan Paul, London 1960.

J.B.Cullingworth, *Housing in Transition: A Case Study of the City of Lancaster 1958–62*, Heinemann, London 1963.

J.B.Cullingworth, *Housing and Local Government in England and Wales*, Allen & Unwin, London 1966.

M.J.Desai, 'An Econometric Model of the World Tin Economy – 1948–61', *Econometrica*, vol. 34, no. 1, January 1966, pp. 105–34.

J.S.Duesenberry, *Business Cycles and Economic Growth*, McGraw Hill, New York 1958.

J.S.Duesenberry, and others (ed.), *The Brookings Quarterly Econometric Model of the United States*, Rand McNally & Co., Chicago, also North Holland Publishing Co., Amsterdam 1965.

J.Duesenberry, O.Eckstein and G.Fromm, 'A Simulation of the United States' Economy in Recession', *Econometrica*, vol. 28, no. 4, October 1960.

M.Duffy, 'A Model of UK Private Investment in Dwellings', unpublished monograph, Econometric Forecasting Unit, London Graduate School of Business Studies, Discussion Paper no. 18, June 1970.

A.W.Evans, 'Private Sector Housing Land Prices in England and Wales', *Economic Trends*, no. 244, February 1974.

M.K.Evans, *Macroeconomic Activity: Theory Forecasting and Control*, Harper Row, New York 1969.

W.S.Forbes, 'A Survey of Progress in Housebuilding', Building Research Station Current Paper 25/69 (unpublished).

C.D.Foster and C.M.E.Whitehead, 'The Layfield Report on the Greater London Development Plan', *Economica*, vol. XL, no. 160, November 1973.

C.D.Foster and C.M.E.Whitehead, 'More Homes of Our Own', *New Society*, 14 March 1974.

C.D.Foster and C.M.E.Whitehead, 'Mortgages', *New Society*, 20 September 1973.

M.Friedman, *A Theory of the Consumption Function*, Princeton University Press, Princeton 1957.

M.Friedman, 'The Role of Monetary Policy', *American Economic Review*, vol. LVIII, no. 1, 1968, pp. 1–17.

G.Fromm, 'Econometric Models of the Residential Construction Sector:

A Comparison', paper presented at The Housing Model Conference for Federal Home Loan Bank Board, Washington DC, March 1971.

G.Fromm and P.Taubman, *Policy Simulations with an Econometric Model*, The Brookings Institute, North-Holland Publishing Co, Amsterdam 1968.

J.Gillies, 'The Future of Federal Housing Policies in the United States', in A.A.Nevitt (ed.), *The Economic Problems of Housing*, Macmillan, London 1967.

J.R.Gould and S.G.B.Henry, 'The Effects of Price Control on a Related Market', *Economica*, vol. XXXIV, no. 133, February 1967.

L.Grebler and S.J.Maisel, 'Determinants of Residential Construction: A Review of Present Knowledge', in D.B.Suits et. al., *Impacts of Monetary Policy*, Research Studies Prepared for the Commission on Money and Credit, Englewood Cliffs, Prentice Hall, New Jersey, 1963, pp. 475–620.

J.Greve, 'Private Landlords in England', *Occasional Papers in Social Administration No. 16*, Bell, London 1965.

W.G.Grigsby, *Housing Markets and Public Policy*, University of Pennsylvania Press, Philadelphia 1963.

Z.Griliches, 'Distributed Lags – A Survey', *Econometrica*, vol. 35, no. 1, January 1967, pp. 16–49.

J.M.Guttentag, 'The Short Cycle in Residential Construction', *American Economic Review*, vol. 51, no. 3, June 1961, p. 292.

P.G.Hall (ed.), *Land Values*, Sweet and Maxwell, London 1965.

A.H.Hansen, *Business Cycles and National Income*, Norton, New York 1951.

W.V.Hole, 'Housing Standards and Social Trends', *Urban Studies*, vol. 2, no. 2, November 1965, pp. 137–46.

A.E.Holmans, 'A Forecast of Effective Demand for Housing in GB in the 1970s', *Social Trends, No. 1*, Central Statistical Office, 1970.

D.S.Huang and M.D.McCarthy, 'Simulation of the Home Mortgage Market in the Late Sixties', the *Review of Economics and Statistics*, vol. 49, no. 4, November 1967, pp. 441–50.

D.W. Jorgenson, 'Rational Distributed Lag Estimates', *Econometrica*, vol. 34, no. 1, January 1966.

D.W.Jorgenson, 'Capital Theory and Investment Behaviour', *American Economic Review*, vol. 53, no. 2, May 1963.

J.H.Kalchbrenner, 'Summary of the Current Financial Intermediary Mortgage and Housing Sectors of the FRB-MIT-PENN Econometric Model', paper presented at the Housing Model Conference for Federal Home Loan Bank Board, Washington DC March 1971.

L.R.Klein, *A Textbook of Econometrics*, Row Peterson & Co., Evanston 1956.

L.R.Klein, 'The Estimation of Distributed Lags', *Econometrica*, vol. 26, no. 4, October 1958, pp. 553–65.

L.R.Klein, R.J.Ball, J.A.Hazelwood and P.Vandome, *An Econometric Model of the UK*, Oxford University Institute of Statistics, Monograph No. 6, Blackwell, Oxford 1961.

L.M.Koyck, *Distributed Lags and Investment Analysis*, North Holland Publishing Co., Amsterdam 1954.

T.H.Lee, 'Demand for Housing: A Cross-Section Analysis', *Review of Economics and Statistics*, vol. 45, no. 2, May 1963, pp. 190–6.

T.H.Lee, 'Housing and Permanent Income: Tests Based on a Three Year Re-interview Survey', the *Review of Economics and Statistics*, vol. 50, no. 4, November 1968, pp. 480–90.

T.H.Lee, 'More on the Stock Demand Elasticities of Non-Farm Housing', the *Review of Economics and Statistics*, vol. 49, no. 4, November 1967, pp. 640–2.

T.H.Lee, 'The Stock Demand Elasticities of Non-Farm Housing', the *Review of Economics and Statistics*, vol. 46, no. 1, February 1964, pp. 82–9.

F.de Leeuw and E.Gramlich, *The Federal Reserve – MIT Econometric Model*, Federal Reserve Bulletin, January 1968, pp. 11–40.

F.de Leeuw, 'The Demand for Housing: A Review of Cross-Section Evidence', *Review of Economics and Statistics*, vol. LIII, no. 1, February 1971.

S.J.Maisel, 'Fluctuations in Residential Construction Starts', *American Economic Review*, June 1963, pp. 359–83.

S.J.Maisel, 'Changes in the Rate and Components of Household Formation', *Journal of the American Statistical Association*, June 1960.

A.J.W.Merrett and A.Sykes, *Housing Finance and Development: An analysis and programme for reform*, Longmans, London 1965.

J.Moreh, 'Aspects of Building Society Finance', unpublished PhD thesis, London University 1967.

R.F.Muth, 'The Demand for Non-Farm Housing', in A.C.Harburger (ed.), *The Demand for Durable Goods*, University of Chicago Press, Chicago 1960, pp. 29–96.

Nationwide Building Society (formerly Co-operative Permanent Building Society), *Occasional Bulletins*, London (irregular), 1953 to date.

L.Needleman, 'Productivity in House-Building', *Lloyds Bank Review*, no. 69, July 1963, pp. 31–40.

L.Needleman, 'A Long Term View of Housing', *National Institute Eco-*

nomic Review, no. 18, November 1961, pp. 19–37.

L. Needleman, *The Economics of Housing*, Staples Press, London 1965.

M.Nerlove, 'Distributed Lags and Estimation of Long-Run Supply and Demand Elasticities: Theoretical Considerations', *Journal of Farm Economics*, vol. 40, no. 2, May 1968, pp. 301–11.

M.Nerlove and K.F.Wallis, 'The Durbin–Watson Statistics in Inappropriate Situations', *Econometrica*, vol. 34, no. 1, January 1966, pp. 235–8.

A.A.Nevitt, (ed.), International Economic Association Conference (1965), *The Economic Problems of Housing*, Macmillan, London 1967.

A.A.Nevitt, *Housing Taxation and Subsidies: A Study of Housing in the UK*, Nelson, London 1966.

R.J.Nicholson and N.Topham, 'Determinants of Investment in Housing by Local Authorities: An Econometric Approach', *Journal of Royal Statistical Society, Series A (General)*, vol. 134, part 3, 1971.

A.R.Nobay, 'Short-term Forecasting of Housing Investment – A Note', *National Institute Economic Review*, no. 41, London, August 1967, National Institute of Economic and Social Research.

C.St J.O'Herlihy and J.E.Spencer, 'Building Societies' Behaviour 1955–70', *National Institute Economic Review*, no. 61, 1972.

D.C.Paige, 'Housing', chapter 12 of W.Beckerman and others, *The British Economy in 1975*, (National Institute of Economic and Social Research, Economics and Social Studies, no. 23), Cambridge University Press, Cambridge 1965.

J.Parry Lewis and D.D.Singh, 'Government Policy and the Building Industry', *District Bank Review*, June 1966.

C.Rapkin, L.Winnick and D.M.Blank, *Housing Market Analysis*, US Housing and Home Finance Agency, Washington, December 1953.

M.G.Reid, *Housing and Income*, University of Chicago Press, Chicago 1962.

J.Revell, 'UK Building Societies', *Economics Research Papers, No. 5*, University College of North Wales, Bangor 1973.

W.J.L.Ryan, *Price Theory*, Macmillan & Co. Ltd., London 1960.

P.Schmidt and R.N.Waud, 'The Almon Lag Technique and the Monetary versus Fiscal Debate', *Journal of American Statistical Association*, vol. 68, no. 341, Applications Section, 1973.

L.B.Smith, 'A Model of the Canadian Housing and Mortgage Markets', *Journal of Political Economy*, vol. 77, no. 5, September/October 1969.

R.M.Solow, *Price Expectations and the Behaviour of the Price Level*, Manchester University Press, Manchester 1969.

I.Stahl, 'Some Aspects of a Mixed Housing Market', Macmillan, London 1967.

M.D.Steuer, R.J.Ball and J.R.Eaton, 'The Effect of Waiting Times on Foreign Orders for Machine Tools', *Economica*, vol. XXXIII, no. 132, November 1966.

P.A. Stone, 'Housing, Town Development, Land and Costs', the *Estates Gazette*, London 1963.

P.A. Stone, *Urban Development in Britain: Standards, Costs and Resources 1964–2004, Vol. I*, Cambridge University Press, Cambridge 1970.

D. Suits, 'Use of Dummy Variables in Regression Equations', *Journal of American Statistical Association*, 52, December 1957, pp. 548–51.

N.Topham, 'Housing Authorities and the Investment Decision', the *Manchester School*, December 1970.

R.Turvey, *The Economics of Real Property*, Allen & Unwin, London 1957.

R.Turvey, 'The Rationale of Rising Property Values', *Lloyds Bank Review*, no. 63, January 1962, pp. 27–41.

UK Central Statistical Office, *Abstract of Regional Statistics*, HMSO, London. Annually.

UK Commissioners of Inland Revenue, *Annual Report*, HMSO, London. Annually.

UK Committee on the Working of the Monetary System (Chairman, Lord Radcliff), *Memoranda of Evidence*, vol. 2, part IV, HMSO 1960.

UK Department of the Environment, *Report of the Committee on the Rent Acts*, (the *Francis Committee*), Cmnd 4609, HMSO, London March 1971.

UK Department of the Environment, *Fair Deal for Housing*, Cmnd 4728, HMSO, London 1971.

UK Department of Trade and Industry, *Family Expenditure Survey*, HMSO, London 1964 to date.

UK Ministry of Health, *Report on Interdepartmental Committee on Rent Restriction Acts* (Ridley Committee) 1937, Cmnd 5621, HMSO, London 1937.

UK Ministry of Health, *Rent Control in England and Wales*, C 133, HSMO 1946.

UK Ministry of Health and Department of Health for Scotland, *Rents – Report of the Inter-Departmental Committee on Rent Control*, Cmnd 6621, HMSO, London 1945.

UK Ministry of Housing and Local Government, *Housing – The Next Step*, Cmnd 8996, HMSO, London 1953.

UK Ministry of Housing and Local Government, *Rent Control – Statistical Information*, Cmnd 17, HMSO 1956.

UK Ministry of Housing and Local Government, P.E.Gray and E.Parr,

Some Effects of the 1957 Rent Act, Cmnd 1246, HMSO, London 1960.

UK Ministry of Housing and Local Government (Central Housing Advisory Committee), *Homes for Today and Tomorrow*, (*Report of a Subcommittee of the Committee*), HMSO, London 1961.

UK Ministry of Housing and Local Government, *Report of the Committee of Housing in Greater London*, (the *Milner Holland Report*), Cmnd 2605, HMSO, London 1965.

UK Ministry of Housing and Local Government, *Old Houses into New Homes*, Cmnd 3602, HMSO, London 1968.

UK Ministry of Housing and Local Government, Scottish Development Department and Welsh Office, *Housing Statistics*, HMSO London. Quarterly.

UK Ministry of Housing and Local Government, *Housing Returns for England and Wales*, HMSO, London. Quarterly.

UK Ministry of Public Building and Works and Department of Employment and Productivity, *Report of the Committee of Inquiry into Certain Matters concerning Labour in Building and Civil Engineering*, Cmnd 3714, HMSO, London, July 1968.

UK National Board for Prices and Incomes, *Pay and Conditions in the Building Industry*, *Report No. 92*, Cmnd 3837, HMSO, London, November 1968.

UK National Board for Prices and Incomes, *Increases in Rents of Local Authority Housing*, *Report No. 62*, Cmnd 3604, HMSO, London 1968.

UK National Economic Development Office, *Construction Industry Prospects until 1970*, report by Joint Working Party, forecasts of the EDCS for Building and Civil Engineering, 1971.

UK Social Survey, *Labour Mobility in Great Britain 1953–63*, Amelia I Harris assisted by Rosemary Clausen, Reports, New Series, SS 333, London 1967.

UK Social Survey, *The Housing Situation in England and Wales in 1964*, Myra Woolf, SS 372, HMSO 1967.

UK Social Survey, *The Housing Situation in 1960*, P.G.Gray and R.Russell, SS 319, HMSO 1962.

UK Social Survey, *The British Household*, P.G.Gray, HMSO, London 1949.

US Congress, 91st Congress, 1st Session, Housing Document No. 91–63, *First Annual Report on National Housing Goals*. 'Message from the President of the US', US Government Printing Office, Washington 1969.

M.J.Vipond, 'Fluctuations in Private House Building in Great Britain

1950–66', *Scottish Journal of Political Economy*, vol. XVI, no. 2, 1969.

C.M.E.Whitehead, 'Some Aspects of the Economics of Housing in the UK', unpublished PhD thesis, London University, 1970.

C.M.E.Whitehead, 'A Model of the UK Housing Market', *Oxford Bulletin of Economics and Statistics*, vol. 33, no. 4, November 1971.

C.M.E.Whitehead, 'Inflation and the New Housing Market', *Oxford Bulletin of Economics and Statistics*, vol. 35, no. 4, November 1973.

L.Winnick, *American Housing and its Use*, Wiley, New York 1957.

M.Wray, 'Building Society Mortgages and the Housing Market', *Westminster Bank Review*, February 1968.

General index

Activity in the building industry 11, 14–15; in US 40n, 61, 64, 68; and bank credit 24, 33, 38–40, 62, 68, 107, 113, 137, 170, 174; long cycles in 61–2
Asset value of dwellings 18–19, 76, 80–2
Autocorrelation 63, 89–91, 109, 120, 122–4, 156–7

Banks: as a source of funds to mortgagors 34, 167; as a source of funds for builders 24, 37–9, 107, 111, 175–6
Building materials, cost 27–8, 107
Building Societies: structure 33, 34; rules relating to mortgagors 35, 81n, 83, 85; effect on housing activity 65; effect on quality of dwellings 35; effect on tenure structure 37; relationship to other financial institutions 178; see also flow of funds to building societies

Capitalisation in the house building industry 23, 33, 38
Clearing costs 26–7
Completions 11, 14–15; actual and simulated 154
Credit restrictions 65, 84; effect on builders 39–40, 64, 107–8; effect on local authority building 24; effect on speed of construction 124–5; see also Activity in the building industry; Flow of funds to building societies

Demolition of buildings 11–14

Econometric models of housing in the UK 65; in US 62–5, 164–5; in Canada 64; cross-section studies 67; limitations 161–4
Employment in the house building industry 22–3, 140, 174; labour only subcontracting (the lump) 23, 29, 107n, 175
Equilibrium in the housing market 69, 81n, 163

Fair rents 16, 17n, 19, 44–5, 51–2
Filtering 61
First purchasers 6n, 19, 83n, 171
Flow adjustment models 77, 87–92, 94–6
Flow of funds to building societies 164–9; and liquidity ratio 36; relationship to price of dwellings 37, 140, 170; relationship to housing demand 84, 91–6, 99, 108, 132, 142; need for modelling 164
Forecasting 63, 131, 139, 145, 148, 151

Housing Associations 48, 51
Household formation 5, 67, 78; headship rates 79

Improvement grants 8, 50–1, 170–1; see also Rehabilitation
Income: elasticity 64–5, 85, 87, 134, 143; data 79; permanent 79
Industrialised building 24
Inflation 51, 54, 68, 76, 80, 82–3, 139, 155, 168–9; effect on demand for housing 89, 134–5, 145; effect on supply of housing 113–15
Insurance Companies 34, 176
Interest rate 64, 82, 154–5, 164, 166, 169, 171; relationship to availability of credit 107; effect on supply 111, 137–8, 140
Investment in housing 21–2

Labour costs in housebuilding 28, 175
Labour productivity in housebuilding 29–30, 31, 107, 175
Lags 60, 162; between starts and completions 24–5, 117–19, 145–6, 156; in demand reaction 69, 87, 178; in supply reaction 69, 172, 178; in inter-relation between finance and housing 177
Land: prices 25–6; relationship to house prices 31, 172–3, 178; relationsip to supply of new dwellings 106–7, 145,

199

Author index